EVERYDAY COMPUTING

improve your skills in easy steps

SECOND
EDITION
★★

JACKIE SHERMAN

First published in 2005 as *Everyday Computer Activities: A step by step guide for older home users*

This second revised edition published in 2008 by Age Concern Books, 1268 London Road, London, SW16 4ER

ISBN: 978 0 86242 440 4

A catalogue record for this book is available from the British Library.

Edited by: Sarah Price.

Page design and typeset by: GreenGate Publishing Services, Tonbridge, Kent.

Printed in Great Britain by: Latimer Trend, Plymouth, Devon.

About the author

Jackie Sherman is currently teaching IT to adults in the community. She also writes computer course materials for distance learning colleges and answers IT queries for various websites and magazines aimed at people over 50.

Jackie graduated in Zoology from Oxford University and worked for the British Council in Ethiopia. She then joined the CBI to work in its education department, before spending 12 years as a university careers adviser. After training as a school teacher, she became involved with several educational research projects before moving into adult basic skills and computers.

Her first book, *Basic Computer Skills Made Simple*, was published by Butterworth-Heinemann in 2001. Her latest book, *Succeed in ECDL*, is published by Hodder Education.

Contents

Part 2: Get the most from your digital camera and scanner 47

Part 3: Make life easier with the internet 73

vii

Introduction

Many people own a computer but don't use it very much, if at all. Perhaps you are in this position: you may not be aware of its possibilities, or you may have found it too difficult to learn how to use properly. Fortunately, things don't have to stay this way.

This book will take you step by step through many of the activities that older people find useful when they start using their computer at home, including working with a digital camera or scanned pictures, playing games, internet shopping, producing labels, sending photos via email, comparing prices and creating greetings cards.

Following these worked examples will help you overcome any reluctance you might have in using your machine, and show you how easy it can be to get the most from your computer.

Nearly all the examples in the book are based on computers running the Windows XP operating system and Microsoft Office 2002 (Office XP) programs, but you will find the screens look very similar if you are running Windows 98, 2000 or ME and the examples will work equally well with earlier or later versions of Microsoft Office.

The screenshots (for example, of the Baby Boomer Bistro on pages 113–115) were taken in spring 2008. You may notice some changes on websites since then.

If you don't have a basic knowledge of computers, or if you may have forgotten something, check out the Appendix first of all for a brief introduction or look through Age Concern's book, *Computing for Beginners* – a more detailed guide for those new to computers. There is also a Glossary at the end of this book to explain technical terms.

Throughout the book, menu options and toolbar buttons are shown in **bold type**.

Get more from your computer

You may already be familiar with using programs such as **Microsoft Word, Excel** and **PowerPoint** – they're the basic packages you find on most computers. However, not everyone realises how much you can do with them. Part 1 looks at just some of the ways you could be getting even more from your computer.

Part 1 covers:

1 Work wonders with Word

- Example 1: Create a word-processed short story and submit it for publication

- Example 2: Create folders to store your work

- Example 3: Design an advertisement for a local newspaper

- Example 4: Print an envelope

- Example 5: Create labels

2 Excel at spreadsheets

- Example 6: Work out your BMI (Body Mass Index) to monitor weight loss

- Example 7: Create and search a family database

3 Personalise your PowerPoint

- Example 8: Create a birthday card using a picture you have taken

Work wonders with Word

Most people who use a computer start by trying their hand at word processing. Letters, invitations and articles look so much more professional, and can be quickly amended and saved.

Starting work

Open your word-processing application by clicking the Word icon 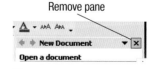 on the Office Shortcut Bar or by selecting **Microsoft Word** from the **Start – All Programs** menu (see Figure 1.1).

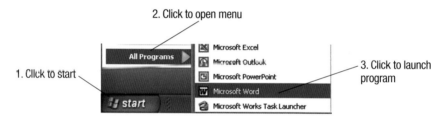

Figure 1.1

Whenever Word opens, it displays a blank page ready for you to start typing. To begin a second piece of work, click the **New** button you can see on the toolbar at the top of the screen ⬜. Note that only commonly used toolbar buttons will be visible on any toolbar. To use one that is not visible, click the down-facing arrow at the end of a toolbar and click **Add or Remove Buttons** to find the missing button (see Figure 1.2).

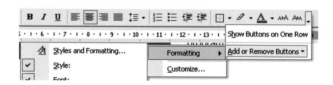

Figure 1.2

You will see a bar down the right-hand side of the screen that is known as the **task pane**. It offers shortcuts to various actions, but it can be removed to give you more room. Either click the **Close** button in the top corner (see Figure 1.3)

Remove pane

Figure 1.3

or open the **View** menu, wait for it to expand fully (or click the double arrows at the bottom to offer all the options) and then click **Task Pane** to take off the tick and remove it from your screen (see Figure 1.4).

Figure 1.4

The flashing black bar on your page – the cursor – shows the position for your text. There is always a margin round the page so that the document will print correctly and a temporary name for your work (Document 1) will show in the title bar (see Figure 1.5).

Figure 1.5

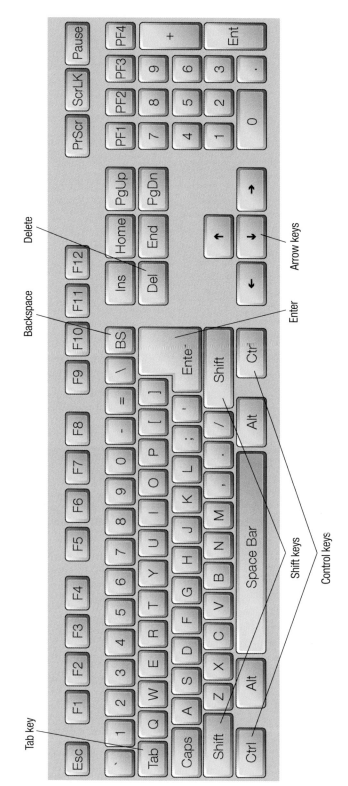

Figure 1.6

If you carry out very little word processing, it's a good idea to get to know some of the special keys on the keyboard before you start (see Figure 1.6):

- *Shift keys* – hold one down as you type a letter and it will appear as a capital or will allow you to type the punctuation symbol at the top of a key; for example @ (above the apostrophe) or % (above the 5).

- *Control keys* – hold one down as you press a letter key to act as a shortcut to common actions; for example with S – save, with P – print, with N – new document, and so on.

- *Enter* – press to move the text insertion point down a line, or to **OK** an action.

- *Arrow keys* – press to move the cursor in that direction.

- *Backspace* – erase text to the left of the cursor.

- *Delete* – erase text to the right of the cursor.

- *Tab key* – found to the left of the letter Q – will move the cursor across the page in short jumps.

Word wrap

After typing some text, such as a title for your work, press the Enter key on the keyboard to move the cursor onto the next line and press it again if you want to leave a blank line before typing the first paragraph.

You do not need to press Enter each time you reach the end of a line within a sentence or paragraph, as the computer automatically moves the next word onto a new line for you. This process is known as **word wrap**.

Correcting mistakes

If you notice that you have made a typing error, move the cursor to the word by clicking the mouse pointer on screen. You can also move the cursor into position by pressing an arrow key in the appropriate direction.

Type new letters, or erase a letter or space that you don't want. Erase to the left of the cursor by pressing the Backspace key and to the right by pressing the Delete key.

We all make silly mistakes and, if you suddenly see that you've typed the same letter several times, or deleted a chunk of your work, click the Undo button ↺. This will step back through your actions – as long as you haven't saved the changes in the meantime.

5

Changing the appearance

To make parts of your work stand out, you can change the appearance of your text by the process known as **formatting**. To type letters in bold type, first click on the **B** toolbar button. You can underline text by clicking the U button, or change to italic typing by clicking the *I* button. Click any of these toolbar buttons again when you are ready to turn off the formatting before continuing. You will know when they are on, as they will display a blue square (see Figure 1.7).

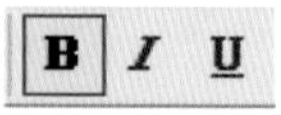

B *I* U

Figure 1.7

There are different types of character (font) you can choose from and a list is available if you click the down-facing arrow in the Font box. You can also increase letter size by selecting an alternative number from the Font size box (see Figure 1.8).

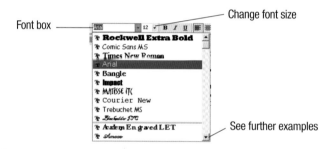

Figure 1.8

Selecting text

If you decide to format your text after it has been typed, select the target text first. Then any formatting will only apply to these words. They will appear as white letters on a black background and you can click an empty part of the screen to take off the selection again.

This is selected text

This is unselected text

There are a number of ways to select text:

- Double-click a word with the mouse pointer.

- Select a line of text by clicking the pointer in the left-hand margin when it shows a right-facing arrow.

- Click and hold down the left mouse button, then drag the pointer across the words or lines.

- If handling the mouse is difficult, click in front of a word and then hold Shift as you press an arrow key to select along the word or text in your chosen direction.

- Select the whole document by opening the **Edit** menu and clicking **Select All** (a shortcut is to hold down the Ctrl key and press the letter A).

Saving

After typing part of your text, it's a good idea to save it. Any work created on a computer is known as a *file*, although files produced using different applications have common names – for example, word-processed files are called *documents*.

Click the **Save** button 💾 to save your document for the first time. This opens the Save As box (see Figure 1.9).

You will find that your first text entry has been selected automatically as the name for your work. This is the name you will see when searching for your work in the future. If this is not what you want the file to be named, change it by clicking in the **File name:** box and typing your preferred text instead.

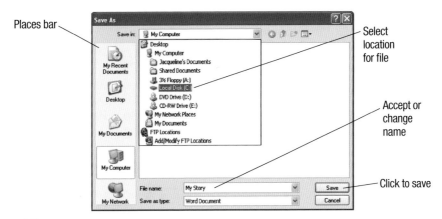

Figure 1.9

You will also be offered the My Documents folder as the location for the file. If you want to save it elsewhere – for example, into a folder on the hard drive – click the drop-down arrow in the **Save in:** box and select an alternative location, or click one of the folders in the left-hand Places Bar (see Figure 1.9). Then click **Save**. You will return to your work and will see that the new file name now appears in the blue title bar.

Updating or Save As

To update your work, taking extra typing or amendments into account and overwriting the original, simply click the **Save** button.

If you want to keep a new version of the document, you need to save it with a new name or in a different location, so that the original is not overwritten. To do this, you must open the Save As box, by going to **File – Save As** and changing the file name and/or location before clicking **Save**.

Closing

Having saved your work, close it at any time by clicking the Close button in the top right-hand corner. The red Close button will exit Word and you will return to the desktop, but the lower button will only close your current document (see Figure 1.10).

Exit Word

Close document

Figure 1.10

Printing

To print one copy of your current document, click the **Print** toolbar button. You may prefer to click the **Print Preview** button first, to check how your document will appear when printed (see Figure 1.11).

Print Preview

Print

Figure 1.11

Close Print Preview to return to the document and make any necessary amendments before printing.

To print several copies of your document, or selected pages only, you will need to open the Print dialog box, so go to **File – Print** and set the various options before clicking **OK** (see Figure 1.12).

Choose which pages to print

Choose how many copies to print

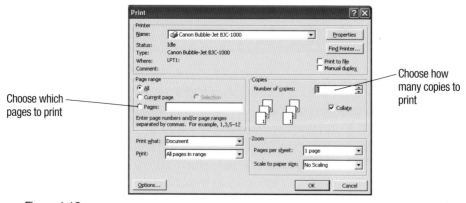

Figure 1.12

8

Example 1

Create a word-processed short story and submit it for publication

One activity that many of us enjoy at any age is writing stories. Many magazines pay £100 to £300 for short stories – particularly those with a twist in the tale – and it can be an enjoyable and lucrative hobby. So here are the steps to follow if you want your short story ready for submission to the editor of your favourite magazine. By following this example you'll also learn some of the slightly more advanced features of Word.

1 If you follow the advice at the beginning of this chapter, you can type your story as a first draft and save it with a suitable name. Most editors want a story of a certain length, so let your word-processing application count the number of words for you. Just open the **Tools** menu and click **Word Count**. You will see the number of words, pages and even paragraphs, characters and lines (see Figure 1.13). A 1,500 word story takes up about four sides of A4.

Figure 1.13

2 Editors like to be able to read your story easily, so it is usual to submit it in double line spacing, with blank lines between each line of text (see Figure 1.14).

Figure 1.14

A quick way to double line space is to select the text and then hold Ctrl and press the number 2 key. Return to single line spacing with Ctrl+1, or 1.5 spacing with Ctrl+5.

You can also use the **Line Spacing** toolbar button (see Figure 1.15).

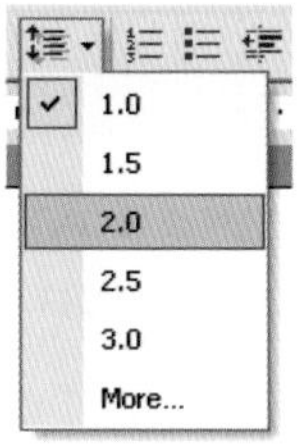

Figure 1.15

3 As you type, you may see red or green lines appearing below some of your words. Red means the word is not listed in the built-in dictionary, and green means that the text is not obeying a common rule of grammar. Green lines will appear, for example, if you leave too few or too many spaces after a comma or full stop. To amend a spelling, right-click the red line to display the menu and select an alternative from the list (see Figure 1.16). For a word that is spelt correctly, such as your name, click **Add to Dictionary** so that it is recognised in future, or **Ignore All** to cancel the error message.

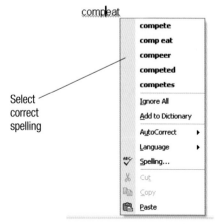

Figure 1.16

Don't forget that the computer will not proofread, so the following sentence will not show any error messages:

He worked a cross to the stares and sit dawn on the bottom steppe. **It should read:** *He walked across to the stairs and sat down on the bottom step!*

4 With a story extending across many pages, you will want to make sure that the pages are clearly labelled, for example, with your name or title of the story and the date, and that there are page numbers on every page. If you add these as a header or footer – repeated entries that appear in the top or bottom margins – they won't affect the page layout.

a Open the **View – Header and Footer** menu and type an entry, such as the story title, in the box that appears. Move across the box by clicking in place with the mouse or pressing the Tab key to add further details and apply formats in the normal way.

b Select entries such as the date or page numbers from the toolbar. They will appear against a grey background and will be updated automatically as you continue to work on your document.

c Add text at the bottom of the page by clicking the Switch Between button and entering more details here (see Figure 1.17).

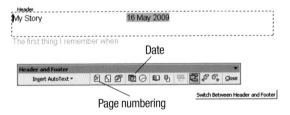

Figure 1.17

d When all entries have been completed, either click the **Close** button on the toolbar or double-click the page text (which will appear grey) to return to the document.

e To remove entries, double-click the header or footer text to open the box, select the entry and press the Delete key.

5 Long documents can look neater if the right-hand edge is straight. This involves **_justifying_** the text. For your front page, or in an accompanying letter, you may want your story title in the centre and your name and address on the right. To reposition any block of text, select it and click the appropriate alignment button on the toolbar (see Figure 1.18).

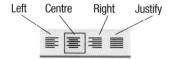

Figure 1.18

Note: Alignment applies to a whole line. After typing and centring a title, for example, press Enter and click the left alignment button if you want the text on the next line to begin at the left margin.

6 Sometimes, you have a change of heart after typing a story. Perhaps your heroine's name doesn't feel right but it has appeared several times on every page. To change all the entries quickly, use Word's Replace tool.

a Open the **Edit** menu and select **Replace**.

b Type the original name in the **Find what:** box and the new name in the **Replace with:** box (see Figure 1.19). If it is straightforward, click **Replace All** and the job is done.

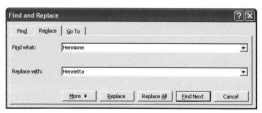

Figure 1.19

c For words where there may be some confusion, or if you want to leave the original in place in your title or on some of your pages, click **Find Next** and check the entry by eye. To replace it, click **Replace**, but to leave it in place and move to the next entry, click **Find Next** again.

7 On a final read-through of your work, you may decide that some sections are in the wrong place. Instead of typing them all out again, you can remove them from the document and store them safely in a part of the computer's memory known as the Office Clipboard. They will stay here until you are ready to *paste* them into their new position, as long as you don't turn off the computer in the meantime.

The process of moving text is known as Cut and Paste. You can carry out Cut and Paste in four steps:

a Select the text to be moved.

> It was a very hot day. I decided not to go out.

b Click the **Cut** toolbar button ✄. The words will disappear. (If you want to copy text to a different position but leave the original in place, you click the **Copy** button 📄 instead.)

c Decide on the new position for the text and click to place the cursor on screen.

> I decided not to go out. |

d Click the **Paste** button 📋. The text appears.

e (This step is optional and you can ignore the button.) Decide whether to apply a new format or retain the original by selecting one of the options offered by clicking the **Paste Options** button 📋 ▾.

8 Once you have printed your story, type an accompanying letter and then send it off. To learn how to add the address to an envelope, see Example 4 below.

Example 2

Create folders to store your work

As you write more and more stories and use your computer for letters and other documents, you will find that your original storage folder becomes too full for you to find individual pieces of work again easily. It may therefore be a good idea to start a file storage system. You can do this within the My Documents folder or, if you use removable disks, on one of these. Eventually, you will build up a large hierarchy of folders that will be much quicker to search.

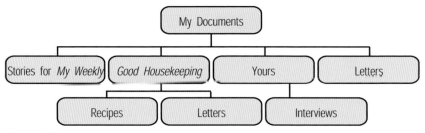

Figure 1.20

1 Open My Computer on the desktop and click the link to My Documents in the task pane, a folder on the C: drive or a writeable CD in the E: drive (see Figure 1.21).

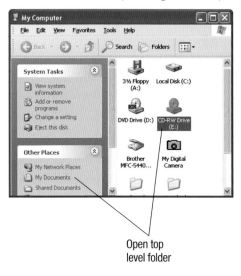

Open top
level folder

Figure 1.21

2 You will see all the documents you have created and saved so far. These can be viewed and reorganised in a number of ways. You can display large or small icons, a list or thumbnails of any pictures. Files can also be organised alphabetically by name or by date created. Change the display by clicking the appropriate option on the **View** menu or **Views** button and change the order by selecting **Arrange Icons by** (see Figure 1.22).

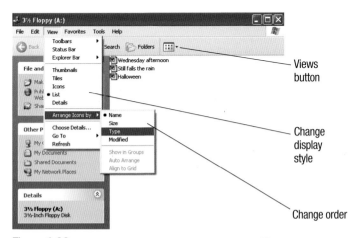

Views button

Change display style

Change order

Figure 1.22

3 Once you have decided how you want to group your files, for example by publication or by topic, click the **File** menu and select **New – Folder** (see Figure 1.23). You could also click the link **Make a new folder** in the task pane.

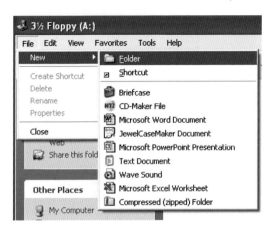

Figure 1.23

4 An empty folder will appear within the window and you
can type its name over the blue text (see Figure 1.24).
(Folders are shown as yellow boxes, whereas files display
the icon for the program used to create them.)

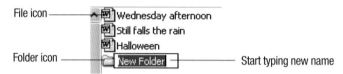

Figure 1.24

5 To move any of the files visible in the window into the
folder, simply click and drag them towards the folder.
When the folder icon turns blue, let go and the file will
be placed inside (see Figure 1.25). You could also select
the file, click the **Move this file** link in the task pane and
choose the correct folder in the window that appears.

Figure 1.25

6 To find a file you have stored inside a folder, you need to
open the folder by double-clicking. The stored file will be
visible inside (see Figure 1.26).

Figure 1.26

7 An alternative method for working with folders is to click
the **Folders** button. This reveals all your folders in the
left pane and the contents of any selected folder in the
right pane. Any folder showing the + symbol will contain

further folders, so click the symbol to open up the folders structure. It will show the - symbol when fully opened (see Figure 1.27). Move files into folders by dragging them across the division between the two.

Click to display folders inside

Reveal folders on your computer

File dragged onto floppy disk

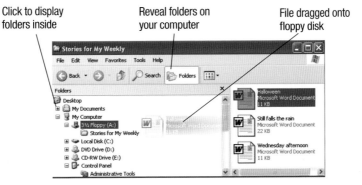

Figure 1.27

8 You can also create folders as you work. Once you have opened the **Save As** window, click the button to create a new folder when the appropriate parent folder is showing in the **Save in:** window. Type its name into the **Name** box, click **OK** and make sure it is showing in the **Save in:** window (see Figure 1.28). You can now save your work directly into this new folder.

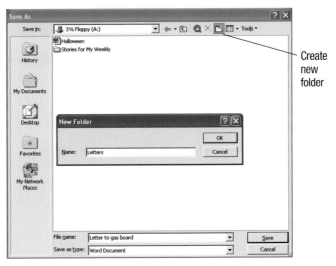

Create new folder

Figure 1.28

Example 3

Design an advertisement for a local newspaper

Once you have mastered the basics of Word, it can be fun to explore the display features. These include setting the text in columns, adding pictures and applying attractive borders. Here is how you could go about designing an advertisement to sell an unwanted fish tank. You will need the Drawing toolbar – if it is not showing along the bottom of the screen, right-click any toolbar and select it from the list.

1. After drafting out the advertisement on paper, you may decide you want it to include a main title and then a description in two short columns. Type all the text normally first of all and then select the description.

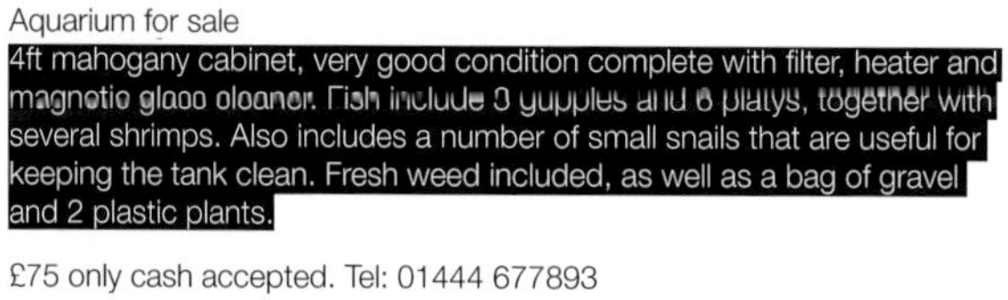

Aquarium for sale
4ft mahogany cabinet, very good condition complete with filter, heater and magnetic glass cleaner. Fish include 3 guppies and 6 platys, together with several shrimps. Also includes a number of small snails that are useful for keeping the tank clean. Fresh weed included, as well as a bag of gravel and 2 plastic plants.
£75 only cash accepted. Tel: 01444 677893

Figure 1.29

2. Open the **Format** menu and select **Columns**. In the dialog box, select the **Two** option and add a tick in the box if you would like to include a vertical line (see Figure 1.30a). Then click **OK** (see Figure 1.30b).

Columns
Presets
One
Two
Three
Left
Right
OK
Cancel
Line between
Number of columns:
2
Width and spacing
Col #:
Width:
Spacing:
1:
6.69 cm
1.27 cm
2:
6.69 cm
Preview
Equal column width
Apply to:
Selected text
Start new column
Two columns
Include line between

Figure 1.30a

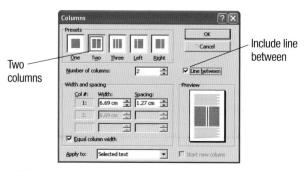

Aquarium for Sale
4ft mahogany cabinet, very good
condition complete with filter,
heater and magnetic glass cleaner.
Fish include 3 guppies and 6
platys, together with several

shrimps. Also includes a number
of small snails that are useful for
keeping the tank clean. Fresh
weed included, as well as a bag of
gravel and 2 plastic plants.

£75 only cash accepted. Tel:014444 677893

Figure 1.30b

3 If the text isn't distributed evenly between the columns when you return to the page, click in front of the first word that you want at the start of the second column, open the **Insert** menu and click **Break**. Select the **Column break** option and then **OK** (see Figure 1.31).

Start new column here

Figure 1.31

4 You can apply different formats to the title, description and contact details, so that the advertisement looks more attractive. You can also centre the title and any other text as necessary and then add a border. For example, select the title, go to **Format – Borders and Shading** and apply a simple or shadowed box with double line style. For a coloured background you could also click the **Shading** tab and select a colour from the palette (see Figures 1.32a and 1.32b).

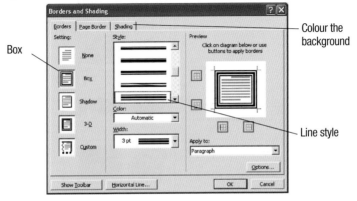

Box

Colour the background

Line style

Figure 1.32a

Aquarium for Sale

4ft mahogany cabinet, very good condition complete with filter, heater and magnetic glass cleaner. Fish include 3 guppies and 6 platys, together with several shrimps.	Also includes a number of small snails that are useful for keeping the tank clean. Fresh weed included, as well as a bag of gravel and 2 plastic plants

£75 only cash accepted. Tel:014444 677893

Figure 1.32b

5 Finally, make the advertisement stand out by adding a picture of a fish. There are two options if you don't take your own photographs: use an image included in Word's Clip Art Gallery or find a picture on the internet.

a *Clip Art*: Click the **Insert Clip Art** toolbar button 🖼 on the Drawing toolbar at the bottom of the screen to open the search pane on the right of your page (see Figure 1.33).
Type in your subject and click **Search**. When the results appear, scroll down to find one you like. To repeat the search with new search words, click **Modify** (see Figure 1.34).

Figure 1.33

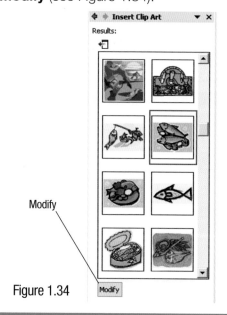

Modify

Figure 1.34

Click a picture you like to add it to the page.

When the picture appears, it may be in the wrong place and the wrong size. To reduce its size, click to reveal the border and move the pointer over a corner box (known as a sizing handle). Drag this inwards when the pointer displays a two-way arrow (see Figure 1.35).

Drag inwards

Figure 1.35

To move the whole picture into position on the page, open the **Draw** menu on the toolbar and select **Text Wrapping – Tight** (see Figure 1.36).

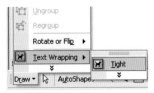

Figure 1.36

This will change the black sizing handles on the border to white circles, and you will now be able to drag the picture with your mouse. Readjust the text if necessary so that the finished advertisement is as you want it (see Figure 1.37).

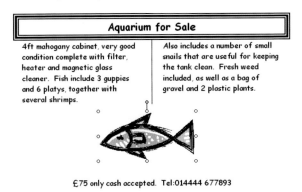

Aquarium for Sale

4ft mahogany cabinet, very good condition complete with filter, heater and magnetic glass cleaner. Fish include 3 guppies and 6 platys, together with several shrimps.

Also includes a number of small snails that are useful for keeping the tank clean. Fresh weed included, as well as a bag of gravel and 2 plastic plants.

£75 only cash accepted. Tel:014444 677893

Figure 1.37

b *Web image*: If you prefer to find a picture on the internet, and you know how to search the internet (see Chapter 8), use a search engine to look for images. Adding clipart in the search box should help ensure that the pictures are free of copyright, but you need to check this before your advertisement is published in a newspaper.

Right-click an image and select **Copy**, return to your advertisement and click **Paste** (see Figure 1.38).

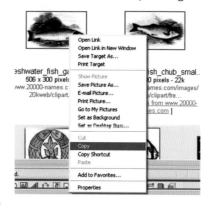

Figure 1.38

You can now carry out the editing, as explained above, to position this picture on your page instead (see Figure 1.39).

Figure 1.39

Example 4

Print an envelope

1 If you have typed a letter that includes the address of the recipient, it is a good idea to use this straightaway to print out an envelope. Simply select the full address and click **Tools – Letters and Mailings – Envelopes and Labels**.

2 Click the **Envelopes** tab and the address will show in the window. You can make changes to it if you need to by clicking in the box (see Figure 1.40).

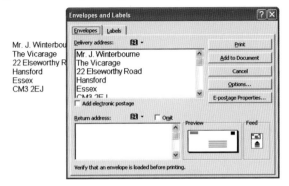

Figure 1.40

3 For unusually sized envelopes, click **Options** and pick a size. Then click the **Printing Options** tab to set the position for the envelope to be fed into your printer (see Figure 1.41).

4 Back in the Envelopes window, click **Add to Document** if you want to keep both envelope and letter together to print later, or click **Print** and print your envelope straightaway.

Figure 1.41

Example 5

Create labels

Word makes printing labels very easy and efficient. You can print the same label many times or create a number of differently worded labels.

To carry out this task, you must first have available special sticky backed label paper, which is available from most good stationers. Each pack will show the label size and will often display a code number. Details of a number of different manufacturers' labels are stored in Word so you can often select the company and then find the exact size or code.

1 To produce a set of different labels, open the Envelopes and Labels window as in Example 4, but then click the **Labels** tab.

2 Find the appropriate label size by clicking **Options** and selecting from the drop-down lists (see Figure 1.42). For unusual sizes, you will need to click the **New Label** button and set the correct measurements yourself.

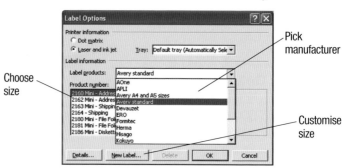

Choose size

Pick manufacturer

Customise size

Figure 1.42

3 Click **OK** and make sure that you check in the main window that you will be producing a sheet of labels, rather than one label in the centre of the page (see Figure 1.43).

Figure 1.43

4 Now click **New Document** and you will see a grid of empty labels on the page. Click in each one and type the name and address or other details – you will only have a few text lines available. Press Enter to move onto a new line and click the mouse or press the Tab key to move to a different label (see Figure 1.44).

Figure 1.44

5 Once you have typed all the labels, either print straightaway or save the document to print another time.

6 To produce a full page of the same label, type the details in the Envelopes and Labels window before printing or clicking **New Document** (see Figure 1.45).

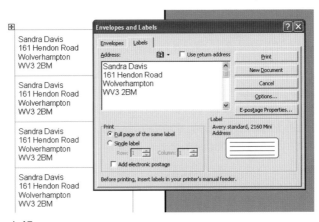

Figure 1.45

Excel at spreadsheets

You may already be familiar with spreadsheets such as Microsoft Excel and the role they can play, for example, in keeping track of weekly shopping expenses or your annual budget. But many people don't use them to their full potential. So in this chapter we look at some of the basic functions and then see how you can use a spreadsheet to check your weight or set up a simple database. These examples may then inspire you to turn to Excel more often in future to help you with the wide range of everyday tasks you are likely to perform.

Spreadsheet programs are excellent for working out complicated sums and playing around with the numbers to see how they affect the results. This is because they perform calculations based on instructions you give them in the form of **formulae**. As long as the formulae contain a reference to the contents of particular cells in a spreadsheet, and not the actual figures, whenever these change the calculations are updated automatically.

Formulae

When you open Excel, you see a vast grid of squares (known as **cells**). Any letters or numbers that you type will automatically appear in the cell that shows a black border. This is the **active cell** and you can click any cell, or press Enter or the Tab key, to activate a different cell.

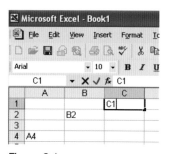

Cells are known by the letter at the top of their column and the number of their row. So cell A4 is in column A and row 4 (see Figure 2.1).

Figure 2.1

To perform a calculation on numbers typed in various cells, for example, to add up the numbers in Figure 2.2, click the cell where you want the answer to appear and then type an = symbol. Excel recognises this as an instruction to perform a calculation.

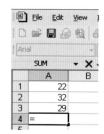

Figure 2.2

- To add numbers, use the + operator.

- To subtract numbers, use the – operator.

- To multiply numbers, use the * operator.

- To divide numbers, use the / operator.

To add up the numbers in cells A1, A2 and A3, click cell A4 and then type:

=A1+A2+A3

The answer appears in the cell when you press Enter, and the formula in any selected cell will be visible in the bar across the top of the sheet known as the Formula Bar (see Figure 2.3).

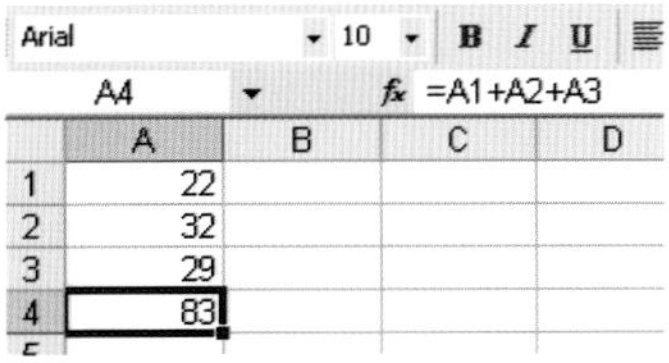

Do not type = 22+32+29 as you will have to edit the formula whenever the numbers are changed.

Figure 2.3

In the same way, to multiply the figure in cell B2 by 20, click the cell where you want the answer to appear (cell C2 in Figure 2.4) and type:

=B2*20

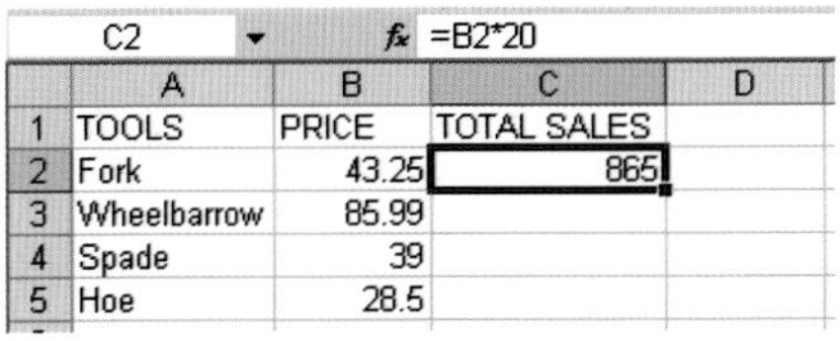

Figure 2.4

Totals

To add up a long column or row of figures, it is quicker to use the automatic tool – the **AutoSum** Σ. Select the full range of cells by dragging across them with the pointer when it shows a white cross ✛. Now click the **AutoSum** button to add the total to the next empty cell (see Figure 2.5).

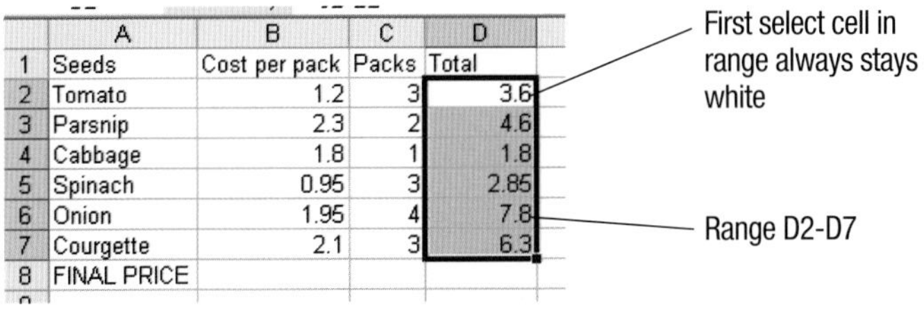

First select cell in range always stays white

Range D2-D7

Figure 2.5

Formatting cell contents

After typing letters or numbers into a spreadsheet, you can change their appearance by selecting them and using the toolbar.

27

Change font type and size, and format entries to **bold**, *italic* or <u>underlined</u> using the toolbar buttons [Arial ▾] [10 ▾] [**B** *I* <u>U</u>] (see Figure 2.6).

	A	B	C	D
1	Seeds	Cost per pack	Packs	Total
2	Tomato	1.2	3	3.6
3	Parsnip	2.3	2	4.6
4	Cabbage	1.8	1	1.8
5	Spinach	0.95	3	2.85
6	Onion	1.95	4	7.8
7	Courgette	2.1	3	6.3
8	FINAL PRICE			26.95
9				

Figure 2.6

For numbers, it is best to open the **Format – Cells** menu and click the **Number** tab. Select the number category – for example currency, percentage, date or number – and, where relevant, set the correct number of decimals or add a symbol or separator. Check the preview before clicking **OK** (see Figure 2.7).

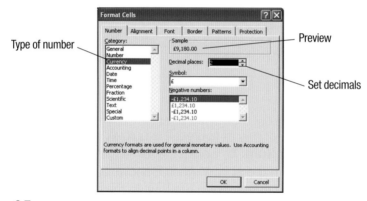

Type of number · · ·　　Preview

· · · Set decimals

Figure 2.7

Saving

Spreadsheet files are known as ***workbooks*** and are saved in the same way as word-processed documents. The equivalent of a page is a worksheet and workbooks can have as many worksheets as you like – just add them from the **Insert** menu. Worksheets are saved automatically when you save the file.

Example 6

Work out your BMI (Body Mass Index) to monitor weight loss

This example is an excellent way to illustrate how you can use Excel to perform complicated calculations. Nowadays, dieters don't rely so much on their exact weight. Instead, a better indication of a healthy weight is provided by the Body Mass Index (BMI). BMI is worked out using a complicated formula related to your weight and height, and the ideal is to be between 20 and 25. The international classification for BMI is:

Below 20: underweight
20–25: acceptable weight
25–30: overweight
30–40: obese
Over 40: very obese

The calculation involves dividing your weight in kilograms by your squared height in metres. As many of us still rely on stones, pounds, feet and inches, this makes the calculation even more complicated.

A computer spreadsheet is an excellent way to keep track of your BMI. As you lose weight, simply enter the new figures into the spreadsheet: the calculation will automatically update to take these into account.

1 Open a new workbook in Excel and enter the headings shown in Figure 2.8 in the cells. Format the entries – for example, to be bold or underlined – if that makes the spreadsheet clearer.

	A	B	C
1	WEIGHT		
2	Stone	Lbs	Weight in lbs
3			

Figure 2.8

2 If you cannot see an entry clearly, widen the column. Do this by moving the mouse pointer to the line between letters at the top of the columns and dragging the border to the right when the pointer shows a two-way arrow (see Figure 2.9). You can also double-click this line to adjust the column width to fit the longest entry exactly.

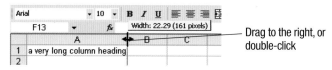

Figure 2.9

3 Type in figures for your weight in cells A3 and B3; for example 9st 13lbs. To work out your weight in lbs, you need to multiply the 9st by 14 and then add the extra lbs. The formula in cell C3 is therefore:

=A3*14+B3

Figure 2.10 shows the result.

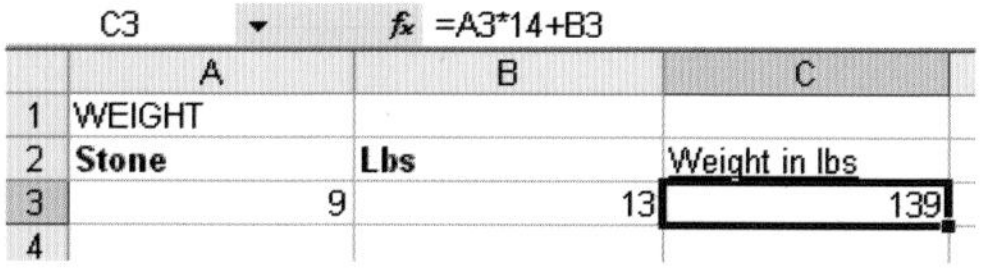

C3	fx =A3*14+B3	
A	**B**	**C**
1 WEIGHT		
2 Stone	Lbs	Weight in lbs
3	9	13	139
4		

Figure 2.10

4 For the BMI calculation you must express your current weight in kilograms. This means dividing the pounds displayed in C3 by 2.2. Add a new heading 'Weight in kilograms' in cell B5 and type the correct formula in cell C5 (see Figure 2.11).

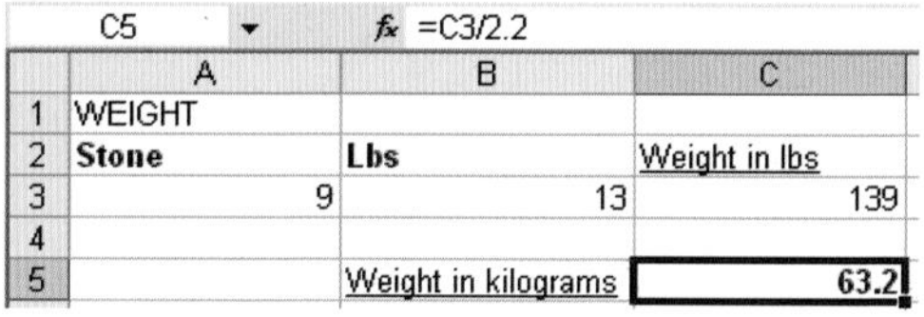

C5	fx =C3/2.2	
A	**B**	**C**
1 WEIGHT		
2 Stone	Lbs	Weight in lbs
3	9	13	139
4		
5	Weight in kilograms	63.2

Figure 2.11

5 Now you need your height in metres: add headings for feet and inches and type in your height, for example 5ft 5ins. Enter a formula to work out the height in inches (multiply the ft by 12 and add the extra inches) (see Figure 2.12).

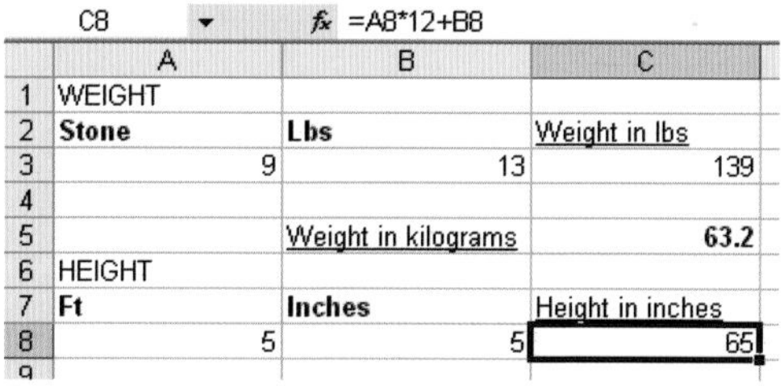

C8	fx =A8*12+B8	
A	**B**	**C**
1 WEIGHT		
2 Stone	Lbs	Weight in lbs
3	9	13	139
4		
5	Weight in kilograms	63.2
6 HEIGHT		
7 Ft	Inches	Height in inches
8	5	5	65
9		

Figure 2.12

6 To express inches in metres, you must multiply the figure by 0.025, so enter the correct formula in cell C10 (see Figure 2.13).

	A	B	C
	C10 ▼	*fx* =C8*0.025	
1	WEIGHT		
2	Stone	Lbs	Weight in lbs
3	9	13	139
4			
5		Weight in kilograms	63.2
6	HEIGHT		
7	Ft	Inches	Height in inches
8	5	5	65
9			
10		Height in Metres	1.6

Figure 2.13

7 To work out the BMI in cell B13, you must square the height measurement (see cell C11) and then divide your weight in kilograms by the squared height in metres. The final spreadsheet will contain the formulae in Figure 2.14.

	A	B	C
1	WEIGHT		
2	Stone	Lbs	Weight in lbs
3	9	13	=A3*14+B3
4			
5		Weight in kilograms	=C3/2.2
6	HEIGHT		
7	Ft	Inches	Height in inches
8	5	5	=A8*12+B8
9			
10		Height in Metres	=C8*0.025
11		Squared metres	=C10*C10
12			
13	BMI	=C5/C11	
14			

Figure 2.14

8 The actual BMI in this case is 24 (see Figure 2.15). As you lose weight, change the entries in cells A3 and B3 and the final BMI will be updated automatically.

	A	B	C
1	WEIGHT		
2	Stone	Lbs	Weight in lbs
3	9	13	139
4			
5		Weight in kilograms	63.2
6	HEIGHT		
7	Ft	Inches	Height in inches
8	5	5	65
9			
10		Height in Metres	1.6
11		Squared metres	2.6
12			
13	BMI	24	

Figure 2.15

9 Keep your spreadsheet safe by clicking the **Save** button and changing the file name from Book1 to 'BMI'.

Example 7

Create and search a family database

As well as performing calculations, spreadsheet programs are very useful for building up databases of information about people or objects, such as record or book collections. One useful database might include friends or members of your family, where you could keep any useful details, such as birthdays, phone numbers, addresses and so on.

1. To create a family database, decide on the main categories under which the information will be stored and set these out as column headings (see Figure 2.16). It is always a good idea to include more rather than fewer headings, in case you need to search for people in a different way. For example, a single column including everyone's full name isn't as useful as two columns holding first names and surnames separately.

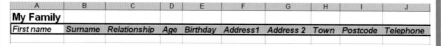

	A	B	C	D	E	F	G	H	I	J
	My Family									
	First name	Surname	Relationship	Age	Birthday	Address1	Address 2	Town	Postcode	Telephone

Figure 2.16

2. If you realise you have forgotten a category, click the column heading letter to the right and go to **Insert – Columns**. A new column will 'slide' into place and you can type in the new heading (see Figure 2.17).

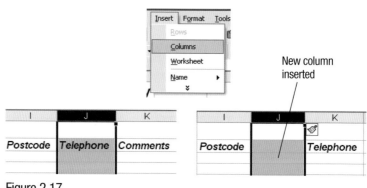

Figure 2.17

3. Start entering everyone's details into your database. You will find that, if you repeat a letter at the beginning of an entry, you may automatically be offered the earlier entry in full (see Figure 2.18). Either press your Tab or Enter key to accept it or keep typing and override the suggestion.

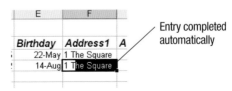

Entry completed automatically

	E	F	
	Birthday	Address1	A
	22-May	1 The Square	
	14-Aug	1 The Square	

Figure 2.18

4. Once you have typed some of the details, save the database to keep the information safe. A complete entry for any one person is known as a **record**. You can add a huge number of records, as each spreadsheet contains thousands of rows.

5. One important aspect of a database is to format the numerical data properly. As long as the program recognises dates and numbers, it can perform calculations and find dates beginning before, after or between those specified, or numbers that are larger or smaller.

6. Any numbers will be placed on the right in a cell, with text appearing on the left. To change the appearance of numerical data but not the underlying values, select all the entries in any column and then go to **Format** – **Cells** – **Number**. Choose **Currency** or **Date**, etc, from the **Category:** list and then set decimal places or number/ date style (see Figure 2.19).

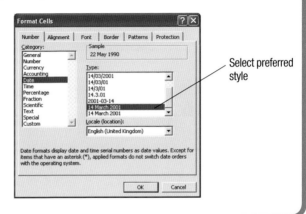

Select preferred style

Figure 2.19

7 Once you have completed all your entries, you are ready to use the database to carry out a search. For example, if you want to see the records for all your brothers, or find if any of your relatives are under 20, select all the main data and open the **Data** menu. Click **Filter** – **AutoFilter** (see Figure 2.20).

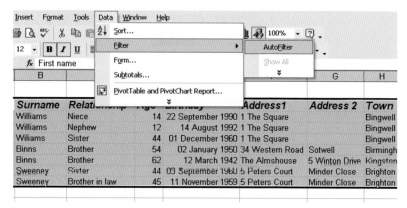

Figure 2.20

8 Arrows appear next to each heading. Click one to display all the entries for that category. For a simple search of matching entries, click one entry – only records that match will be displayed (see Figure 2.21).

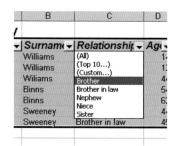

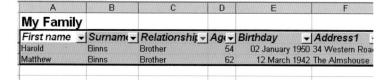

Figure 2.21

9 Before carrying out a new search, click **(All)** in the category you have previously searched to show all the records again or select the **Show All** option from the **Data** – **Filter** menu. In some cases, you may prefer to carry out a second search based on this subset of your database to refine the search further.

10 For searching that relies on a calculation or logical statement rather than an exact match, click the **(Custom)** entry for any category, for example in the Age column. You can now set the criteria for searching for teenagers. Choose options such as **less than** or **greater than** from the drop-down menus and, if necessary, type your own figures in the boxes (see Figure 2.22).

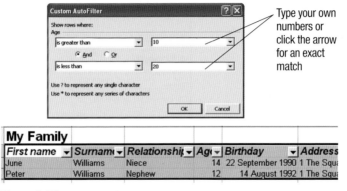

Type your own numbers or click the arrow for an exact match

Figure 2.22

11 To find records where an entry is not known in full, choose **begins with** or **contains**, or use the * for the unknown characters (see Figure 2.23).

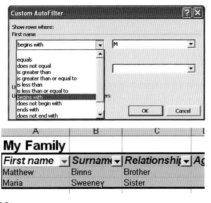

Figure 2.23

12 A final function that may make your database more useful is to reorder (**sort**) all the records, for example by town, surname or age. Take off the filter mechanism by selecting **Data** – **Filter** and clicking **AutoFilter** to remove the tick, but keep the data selected. Now you can select the **Sort** option from the same menu.

13 Decide on the order of your sort – for example, first by Surname and then by First Name – and make these selections from the boxes (see Figure 2.24). Check that you are sorting in the correct order – alphabetical, from lowest to highest is Ascending, and from highest to lowest is Descending – and then click **OK**.

Secondary sort | First level sort

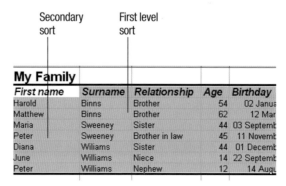

My Family				
First name	*Surname*	*Relationship*	*Age*	*Birthday*
Harold	Binns	Brother	54	02 Janua
Matthew	Binns	Brother	62	12 Mar
Maria	Sweeney	Sister	44	03 Septemb
Peter	Sweeney	Brother in law	45	11 Novemb
Diana	Wiliams	Sister	44	01 Decemb
June	Williams	Niece	14	22 Septemb
Peter	Williams	Nephew	12	14 Augu

Figure 2.24

Personalise your PowerPoint

The principal use of the software package PowerPoint is to make presentations to audiences both small and large; it allows images to be combined with text helping to give emphasis to the message being put forward. The package allows the use of photographs, graphics and text adding an extra dimension to any presentation.

PowerPoint can also be used in a similar way to desktop publishing software. By using it to create a greetings card you will learn many of the advanced features this software has to offer.

If you do not have a digital camera or scanner and want to use someone else's pictures, you have three choices: use a copyright-free image provided on a CD-ROM; use the Clip Art available with Microsoft Office applications (see Example 3 starting on page 18); or find a picture on the web (searching the web is explained in Chapter 8).

Should you want to find a picture on the web, type the subject of your picture into the search box at any search engine website and, if available, select an image-only search (see Figure 3.1). For more about finding things on the web see page 74.

Search for pictures only

Figure 3.1

If you include the Word Clip Art in the search box, you should find images free of copyright that you can use in your cards. Click a small image to see further details and, when it opens, click the link to see it full size (see Figure 3.2).

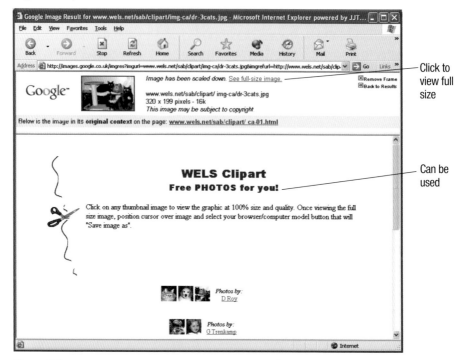

Click to view full size

Can be used

Figure 3.2

You can now either copy it straight from the website into your card or save it onto your computer to insert later. To save the picture, right-click the image and select **Save Picture As** (see Figure 3.3). The **Save As** window will open and you can name and save the file as normal. If you choose **Copy**, make your card as explained below and, at any stage, right-click the slide and select **Paste** to add the picture.

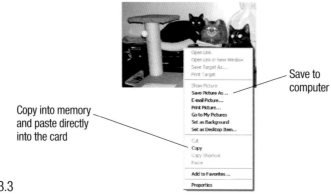

Save to computer

Copy into memory and paste directly into the card

Figure 3.3

Example 8

Create a birthday card using a picture you have taken

For a simple one-fold card using A4 paper, the whole card will be printed out on a single piece of paper that will then need to be folded correctly. (Once this technique has been mastered, you can buy blank cards, set the page size to A5 or A6 and create any inside text after printing the front first.)

Set out your A4 card as in Figure 3.4.

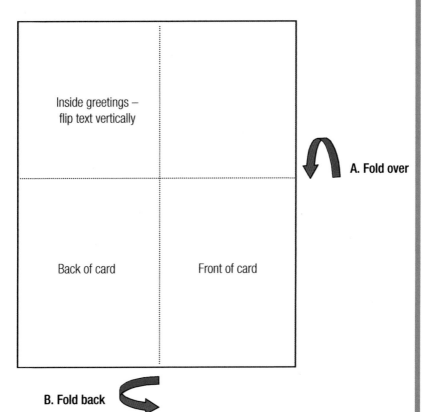

Inside greetings – flip text vertically

A. Fold over

Back of card　　Front of card

B. Fold back

Figure 3.4

1　Open PowerPoint by clicking the icon or selecting it from the **Start – All Programs** menu. Your 'page' is referred to as a *slide* and a slide appears automatically.

2 This first slide arrives with boxes already displayed for you to enter your text into, but to make a card you will want a blank slide. Go to **Format – Slide Layout** (see Figure 3.5).

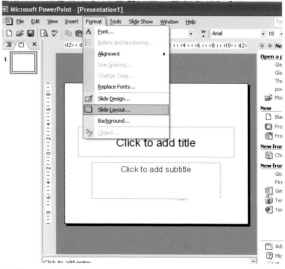

Figure 3.5

3 Select a blank slide layout from the list and click to apply it to your slide (see Figure 3.6).

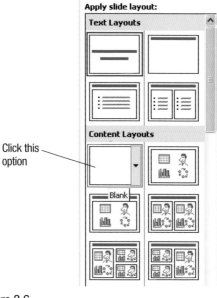

Figure 3.6

4 The slides are in landscape orientation, which will allow you to create a card that folds from the top. If you want a card with a book (sideways) fold, open the **File – Page Setup** menu and change to Portrait orientation (see Figure 3.7).

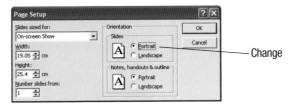
Change

Figure 3.7

5 You are now ready to design the front of the card. To help you work within the relevant sectors of the slide, add non-printing guidelines from the **View – Grid and Guides** menu (see Figure 3.8).

Add guidelines

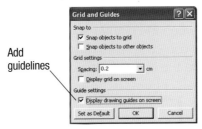

Figure 3.8

6 To include any image saved on your computer, go to **Insert – Picture – From File** or click the **Insert Picture** button on the Drawing toolbar and locate your picture. Select it, click **Insert** and it will appear on the slide. It will probably be far too large, so move your mouse over a corner white sizing circle, hold down the left button and drag the boundary inwards when the pointer changes to a two-way arrow. Let go and the picture will be much smaller (see Figure 3.9).

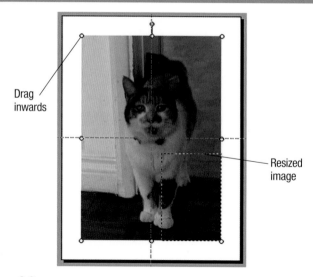

Figure 3.9

7 Continue to adjust the size if necessary and then drag the picture into position in the bottom, right-hand quarter of the slide when the pointer shows a four-way arrow. If appropriate, you could also drag the green circle left or right to rotate the image (see Figure 3.10).

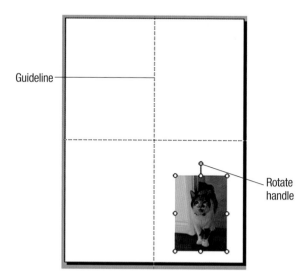

Figure 3.10

8 Now you can add some text to the front of the card. You have two choices: normal text typed into a text box or a WordArt object:

a Text box: Click on the **Text Box** button and drag the mouse across the slide when the pointer shows a cross. This will create a small box with the cursor inside and you can start typing straightaway (see Figure 3.11). Note that you will need to increase the text font size in order to fill the space as you cannot simply stretch the box.

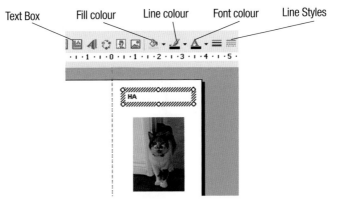

Figure 3.11

Colour the letters by selecting from the **Font Colour** drop-down arrow and add coloured borders or fill (background shading) to the Text Box from other Drawing toolbar buttons (see Figure 3.12).

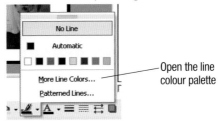

Figure 3.12

Change the style, size, position and appearance of the text using the formatting toolbar buttons (see Figure 3.13) or **Format** – **Font** menu options.

Figure 3.13

Finally, adjust the position of the box so that it is centred above your picture, and add a second box underneath if you want more text on the front of the card (see Figure 3.14).

Happy Birthday

Figure 3.14

b WordArt: Click the **WordArt** button on the Drawing toolbar to add a text object that can be shaped, stretched and coloured. Select your preferred font style from the gallery (see Figure 3.15) – although you can change it later.

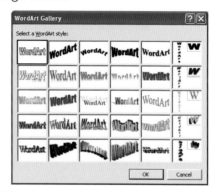

Figure 3.15

Type the text for the card and click **OK** (see Figure 3.16).

Figure 3.16

Make other changes from the toolbar that will appear whenever the WordArt is selected (see Figure 3.17).

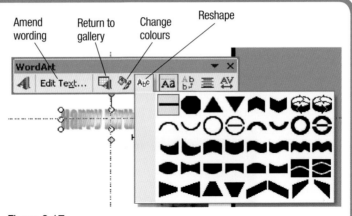

Figure 3.17

Resize and move the WordArt so that it fits the space above your picture (see Figure 3.18).

Figure 3.18

9 Repeat the addition of WordArt, text boxes and pictures for the back and inside of the card. So that the words can be read, however, you will need to flip any inside text vertically by selecting this option from the **Draw – Rotate or Flip** toolbar menu (see Figure 3.19). You could also position the pointer over the green circle on the rotate arm and drag the words round 180°.

Figure 3.19

10 When the card is complete, print it onto normal paper or specially purchased greetings card or photographic paper (see Figure 3.20). If not straightforward A4 size, make sure that you position the text and pictures appropriately. (Some greetings card packs will even include software to help you position the contents, add text and print correctly.)

Figure 3.20

Get the most from your digital camera and scanner

More and more people nowadays have digital cameras and for good reason. Not only will they work out cheaper than conventional ones (no need to buy film ever again) you can also do a lot more with your pictures. Part 2 looks at what you can do if you have a computer and a digital camera. It also includes an example of how to use a scanner, as these are now commonly available and often built into modern multifunctional printers.

Part 2 covers:

4 Digital cameras explained
- Example 9: Take a picture of your pet, store it on your computer and print out a copy

5 Create CDs with ease
- Example 10: Store backup copies of your pictures on a CD

6 Simply scan it and add it
- Example 11: Scan a painting and add it to a poster

7 Bring your photos back to life
- Example 12: Restore an old photo

CHAPTER 4

Digital cameras explained

Once you have used a digital camera, you will find it very hard to return to a conventional one. Not only can you see small 'thumbnails' of your pictures as soon as they are taken, you need never buy film again. Simply save the pictures you want to keep onto your computer, discard the rest and use the camera over and over again.

Once the pictures are on your computer, you can use image-editing software to change any parts you don't like and the improved pictures can then be stored on disk, sent via email to relatives and friends, or printed out. Using high-quality photographic paper will allow you to produce prints as good as those that, in the past, you might have collected from Boots or Bonusprint.

For more detailed guidance on using a digital camera, see *Your Digital Camera Made Easy* also published by Age Concern.

Resolution

The major consideration when using a digital camera is its resolution. This is the measure of how much detail shows in a picture (ie the sharpness of the image) and relates to the number of dots of colour (**pixels**) per inch (**ppi**). As the pixel number is fixed, the more you enlarge a picture, the less clear it becomes until, like newsprint, you start to see each dot that makes up the image. It is therefore important to consider how sharp you want your picture to be when it is printed at a particular size. For most purposes, you should try to print your picture at a resolution of 300 ppi.

When it comes to buying a digital camera, you will find them described as having a resolution of between 2 and 10 megapixels. For example, an inexpensive digital camera with a resolution of 3 megapixels will produce images containing 2,000 x 1,500 pixels, and will print out good quality pictures 7″ x 5″ (18 cm x 12.5 cm) and even quite satisfactory pictures 8″ x 6″ (20 cm x 15 cm) in size.

You have to strike a balance between how sharp you want your final images to be and the size of the image file, because large, high-resolution images are slower to work with and take up more room on your computer.

Software

Before you can see the pictures on your computer, you need to insert the CD-ROM and follow the instructions to install the software that will have come with your camera. You may prefer to install more advanced image-editing software, such as Paint Shop Pro or PhotoShop, which will enable you both to work with your camera images and carry out more sophisticated editing. You can find out more about using one of these programs in Example 12 on page 67.

Example 9

Take a picture of your pet, store it on your computer and print out a copy

It is important to read the manual that came with your camera and get to know your own digital camera settings before starting this example.

1 Your camera should be ready to use straightaway, as all it requires is a battery and the **Image Memory Card** that enables you to record the digital images electronically and store them until you are ready to transfer them onto a computer. Turn on the camera, make sure that the dial is set to still photography (usually showing a coloured camera symbol: see Figure 4.1) and then aim, focus and release the shutter exactly as you would when using a conventional camera to take pictures.

Figure 4.1

2 Take a few pictures of your pet from different angles, or use the zoom, and then, if you want to, preview them on the camera. Change the dial to playback mode (usually showing a solid arrow symbol) and press the forward and backward arrows on the camera to move through the images. At this point, if you want to take more pictures and you have not bought an extra large memory card, you could erase unwanted images by clicking the menu button and choosing the Delete option.

3 When you have finished taking pictures of your pet and want to view them properly, you need to download them onto your computer. There are two main ways you can do this:

a Turn off the camera and connect it to your computer with the USB cable that has been provided. Plug one end of the cable into the camera and the other into a spare USB slot (a free point for connecting extra hardware items) at the back, or sometimes the front, of your computer (see Figure 4.2).

To camera

To computer

Figure 4.2

b As an alternative, remove the memory card from the camera and fit it into a card reader that can then be plugged directly into a USB slot of your computer.

4 If using a cable, turn on the camera, and your software may start up automatically. If not, find it from an icon on the desktop or the **Start – All Programs** menu and click the appropriate disk or folder in the left-hand list.

5 All the pictures on the camera's memory card will be displayed as small, medium or large ***thumbnails***. In the folders list, the camera will show as a separate drive alongside the floppy disk and CD-ROM drives – perhaps named something like 'Removable Disk E:' – and you may need to open one or more subfolders to locate your images (see Figure 4.3).

Find camera and folder containing the pictures

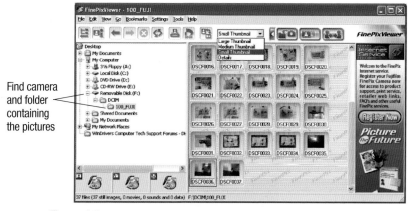

Figure 4.3

6 One option when viewing pictures is to click the **Slide Show** toolbar button (see Figure 4.4) and watch them that way. The toolbars and menus will disappear, and you will see each picture in full-screen mode. Wait as the next picture is revealed or click the mouse to exit or delete a particular image.

Figure 4.4

7 Double-click any thumbnail image to open it fully. You can now carry out some basic editing using the toolbar provided (see Figure 4.5).

Add text   Zoom in or out

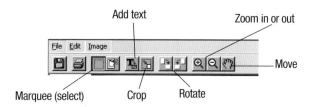

Move

Marquee (select)   Crop   Rotate

Figure 4.5

Most types of software have similar tools. For example, you can cut off unwanted parts by clicking on the **Marquee (select)** button, drawing round the area of the picture you want to keep and then clicking the **Crop** button (see Figure 4.6). Alternatively, click the **Crop** button first, draw round the part of the image you want to retain with the pointer and then double-click the mouse inside your selection.

Select area to keep

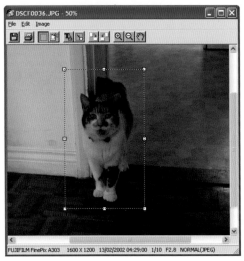

Cropped picture

Figure 4.6

Rotate your image left or right by clicking the appropriate **Rotate** button, and add text by clicking on the **Text** button and then typing in the box that appears. After clicking **OK**, move the text to an appropriate position with your pointer.

8 For images you want to keep, click the **Save** button or go to **File – Save As** and make sure that you change any numbered file name to one that is more memorable (see Figure 4.7).

Figure 4.7

9 You may be directed to save images in a folder labelled My Pictures, within the My Documents folder automatically set aside for saving all your work, but you can always choose an alternative location if you prefer. Click the arrow in the **Save in:** box and select a different drive or open a folder showing in the **Save As** window (see Figure 4.8).

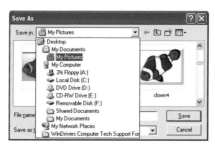

Figure 4.8

10 If you want to open your pictures directly into an image-editing program, open the program, click **File – Open** or **Browse** and open the camera folder to view thumbnails of the images. Double-click any picture to view, save or start making changes.

11 To print a good quality picture, you will need to buy photographic paper from a high street stationer or via the internet. You can even buy packs of photo greetings cards that have a glossy coating and can be folded. They will come with appropriately sized envelopes and may also include software that helps you position your picture correctly on the page (see Example 8 on creating a birthday card on page 39).

12 Open the picture and go to **File** – **Print** or click the **Print** toolbar button to display the printer settings dialog box. Click **Properties** and select the correct paper and colour settings before clicking **OK** (see Figure 4.9).

Figure 4.9

13 Sometimes you may want to print several images on a single piece of paper or produce different sized prints. If you open your pictures using Windows Picture and Fax Viewer (select by right-clicking and choosing **Open with ...**), you can click the **Printer** icon and then use the **Photo Printing Wizard** to take you through the setup (see Figure 4.10).

Click for Wizard

Figure 4.10

14 Select **Contact Sheet Prints** for this option, or choose from a range of printing sizes (see Figure 4.11).

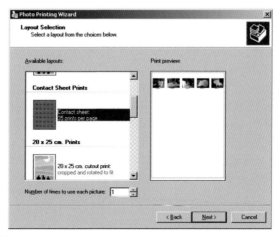

Figure 4.11

Creating CDs with ease

As you start producing documents, using your digital camera or visiting websites to find information or music that you want to keep, you will need to save copies of your files somewhere safe. Most of the programs you use will be saved onto the hard disk inside your computer, on the C: drive. Any files that you create are usually saved automatically in an area of the disk labelled My Documents. Pictures will be saved in a subfolder labelled My Pictures and, as you saw in Example 2, you can create a range of different folders if you want to group certain types of file together.

Soon, you will find that you need extra storage space – perhaps for files you aren't sure you want to keep but are not ready to delete, or for backup copies of important files in case your computer crashes and you lose the originals.

Most modern computers have drives that can read multimedia CD-ROMs and music CDs or DVDs. These drives can store large amounts of data and many people now create their own disks as a form of extra storage. Some computers have a built-in CD or DVD-Writer. If yours does not, you will need to buy one that can be attached externally. These writers work by using a laser to **burn** files onto the optical disk.

The software needed to create the disks is already installed on Windows XP machines but, for older operating systems, there are a range of programs that you can buy including Nero, Roxio Easy CD Creator and Pinnacle Instant CD.

CD-R or CD-RW?

There are two main types of disk that can be used in CD-Writers:

- **CD-R** stands for CD-Recordable and these disks can only be written to once. When they are full, you cannot erase or write over the files. However, they are usually quite cheap to buy and can be read by most CD–ROM drives and audio CD players.

- **CD-RW** stands for CD-Rewritable as these disks allow you to amend files and rewrite to them many times. They cannot always be read by standard CD-ROM drives and may be a little more expensive than CD-Rs and so are best used when you want to work regularly on your files. Once you have enough material and won't want to make any more changes, transfer the files to CD-Rs for long-term storage.

Example 10

Store backup copies of your pictures on a CD

1. Place a new CD-R or CD-RW in the CD drive and wait for the dialog box to open on screen. The selected option will be to view the contents of the disk, so either click **OK** to see what is already on the disk or click to take no action at this stage (see Figure 5.1).

Figure 5.1

2. For a new disk that you choose to open and view, nothing will show. You now need to locate the files you want to copy. Click the up arrow or any link to My Pictures or the folder location and browse through your files to locate your pictures (see Figure 5.2).

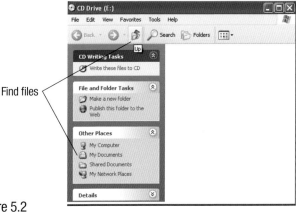

Figure 5.2

57

3 When you reach the appropriate folder, select a picture by clicking it with the mouse. You can select several pictures by holding down the Ctrl key as you click each one. When all the pictures you want to save onto the CD have been selected, click the menu option **Copy the selected items** in the Picture Tasks Pane (see Figure 5.3).

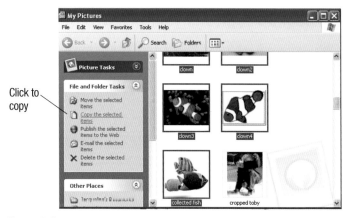

Click to copy

Figure 5.3

4 Find the CD Drive in the list and click Copy (see Figure 5.4).

Figure 5.4

5 In a few minutes, you may see a small balloon label appear at the bottom of the screen showing that your files are waiting (see Figure 5.5). Either click this or simply re-open the E: drive to see your files displayed ready for writing to the CD. They will appear paler than any files that have already been copied to the disk.

Select the option **Write these files to CD** and, if you want to, name the disk when asked to do so (see Figure 5.5). Its default name is the first date files were written to it.

Figure 5.5

6 Click **Next** and the files will start to be copied (see Figure 5.6).

Figure 5.6

7 At the end of the writing process, your disk will be ejected from the drive so that you can label it and put it away for safe keeping.

Simply scan it and add it

Scanners allow you to capture pictures, text or drawings from the printed page and convert them into computerised information that you can then work with. Scanners vary in price from £40 to over £250, with some models also doubling as printers/photocopiers. If you want to turn printed words into word-processed text, you will need to ensure that your scanner includes **OCR** (Optical Character Recognition) software.

The most versatile scanners are known as **flat bed** because you lay the page face down on a glass plate housing the scan head and can scan bulky objects by leaving off the cover of the machine. The scan head is made up of hundreds of light-sensitive sensors, together with a light source, mirrors to reflect the image, filters and a lens. The picture is created by the scan head moving slowly across the document on a belt attached to a motor.

As with digital cameras, resolution is important because it relates to the sharpness of the final image. Resolution is determined by the number of sensors. To produce images with a resolution of 300 × 300 dots per inch (dpi), the scanner will have several thousand sensors, but some scanners use software to **interpolate** extra dots (pixels) between those actually scanned to add perceived detail to the image.

If you buy a new scanner, connect it to your computer and then use the disk provided to install the software that will control the machine and enable you to work with your images.

Example 11

Scan a painting and add it to a poster

It is important to read the manual and get to know your own scanner settings before starting the example. As scanner menus can look very different, this example uses images from two different programs – Hewlett Packard Director and Image-In Color.

1 Lay your picture face down on the scanning plate and open the software program. There may be an icon on the desktop (as in Figure 6.1). If not, you will need to find the program from the **Start** – **All Programs** menu.

Figure 6.1

2 Click the button that starts the process, for example **Scan** (see Figure 6.2) or **Import** – **TWAIN** – **Acquire**. (*TWAIN* is a standard that allows image-editing programs to acquire images from a range of scanners.) There may be extra options, such as using your scanner as a photocopier.

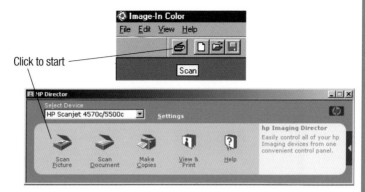

Figure 6.2

3 You may need to click a **Prescan** or **Preview** button, or you may automatically see the image in preview mode. This will allow you to set up the scanner for your particular image (see Figures 6.3, 6.4 and 6.5).

a Reduce the size of the target image by dragging in the boundaries if you don't need the whole page scanned.

b Select the type of image you want to produce – black and white, greyscale or colour.

c Use the toolbar buttons, menus or panel settings to amend the contrast and brightness and set an appropriate resolution: text below 300 dpi may look grainy and be hard to read but coloured images may be quite acceptable at a lower resolution.

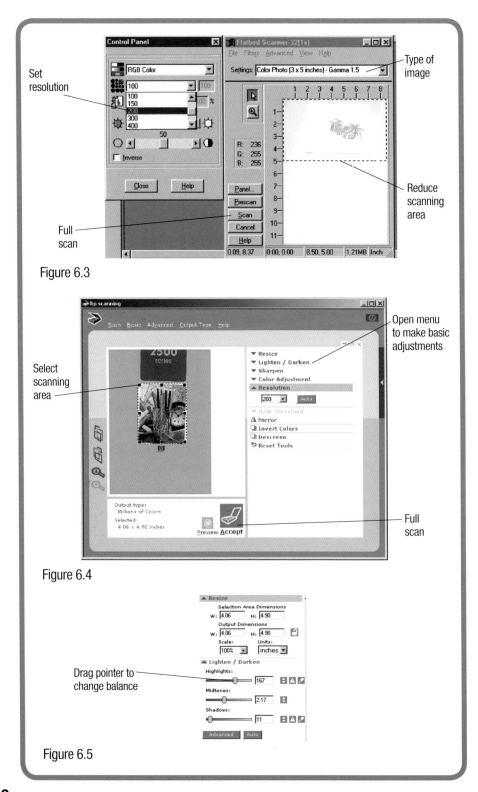

Set resolution

Full scan

Figure 6.3

Type of image

Reduce scanning area

Select scanning area

Open menu to make basic adjustments

Full scan

Figure 6.4

Drag pointer to change balance

Figure 6.5

4 Click the button to scan your image. The higher the resolution, the slower this process will be (see Figure 6.6).

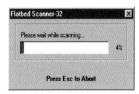

Figure 6.6

5 Eventually, your picture appears on screen. Depending on your software, you can either work on it directly or will need to double-click it to open your editing package. Change the magnification if necessary to view the whole document properly (see Figure 6.7).

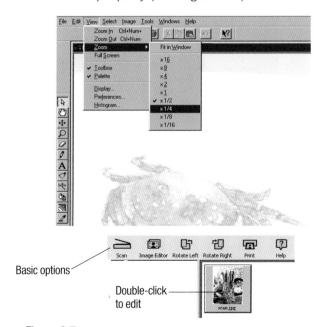

Basic options

Double-click
to edit

Figure 6.7

6 Use any of the tools available to make changes. For example, change the colours, add text or select parts with the selection arrow and click **Crop** to remove unwanted areas of the picture (see Figures 6.8 and 6.9).

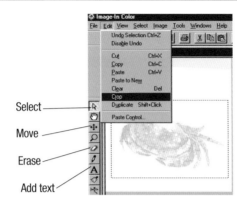

Select

Move

Erase

Add text

Figure 6.8

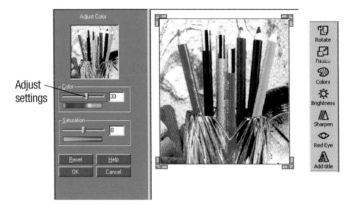

Adjust
settings

Figure 6.9 (HP)

7 To keep the image safe, it's a good idea to save it before making any changes. Your system may be set to save scanned images as a particular image file type (such as .tif), but you should be able to choose a compressed format that will save space (such as .jpg files) (see Figure 6.10).

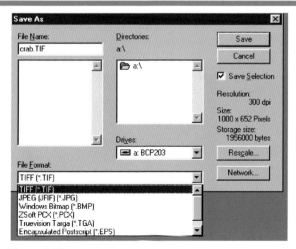

Figure 6.10

8 To copy the scanned picture into a Word document (or other application you may want to work with, such as PowerPoint), use the selection tool or menu to select all or part of the image and then click the **Copy** button. Open your new document (you can minimise or close the scanning software window first), right-click on the page and select **Paste**.

9 To produce a poster, it is easiest to use PowerPoint. After your scanned picture has been pasted onto a slide, adjust its size and position (see Example 8 on creating a birthday card on page 39). Colour the page by selecting **Format** – **Background** and choosing a colour from the drop-down list in the box (see Figure 6.11).

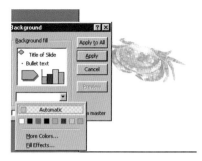

Figure 6.11

65

10 Add text in a text box or as WordArt and then click the **Print** button to print out a copy of your poster (see Figure 6.12).

Villa Fleur

For the holiday of a lifetime

Figure 6.12

Bring your photos back to life

Do you have treasured old photographs that are looking a little the worse for wear? Perhaps they are scratched, the colours have faded, or they are even torn in places. Fortunately, you can now combine the use of a scanner and special editing software to make them look nearly as good as new.

You will need to install a dedicated computer program for this activity. Such programs are called graphics or image editors. You can buy cut-down versions of the expensive professional editions or download trial copies; they all work in a similar way. Some commonly available packages include Corel Paint Shop Pro and Adobe PhotoShop Elements.

There are so many tools and special effects that it can take many weeks to master them all. However, here are some simple effects that you can apply using the automatic settings.

Example 12

Restore an old photo

1. Once you have installed your software, open it and scan in your photo directly or open any scanned image into the program. We will use Paint Shop Pro for this example.

2. The image appears in its own window inside the Paint Shop Pro workspace (see Figure 7.1) and, if not yet saved, save it now just in case the changes you make need to be repeated or cancelled. It is a good idea to save it in the software's own file type (for example .psp for Paint Shop Pro) so that you can work on it using all the tools available. (Note that saving a jpeg file removes some detail *each time you save*, so try to limit the number of times you save such files anyway.)

   To zoom in and view parts of the picture in more detail, press the + key on the keyboard, and zoom out by pressing the –.

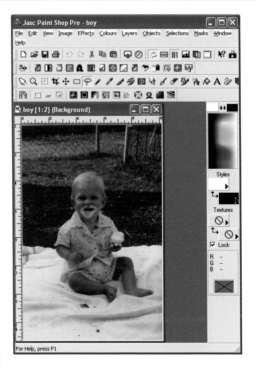

Figure 7.1

3 *Scratch removal*: If there are scratches, or scratched areas, draw round them using one of the selection tools: the square shape selects standard areas and the lasso allows you to draw round unusual shapes. Once selected, a flashing dotted line (a marquee) shows the selected area (see Figure 7.2).

Figure 7.2

Now open the **Effects** menu, select **Enhance Photo** and click **Automatic Small Scratch Removal**. This will open a dialog box showing 'before' and 'after' images so that you can see the effect of any changes. If your scratch is not camouflaged well enough by the automatic settings, change some of these manually. Preview the whole picture by clicking the **Proof** button (see Figure 7.3). When settings are acceptable, click **OK** and when you are back in the photo, double-click on the screen or go to **Selections** – **None** to remove the marquee.

Proof button to preview picture

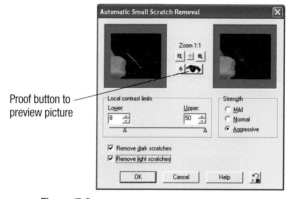

Figure 7.3

4 *Repairing tears*: These normally show as white areas, and the best way to remove them is to 'paint' over them with another part of the image, such as sky or grass. This process, which is known as ***cloning***, is equally useful for camouflaging objects in the picture that you don't want, such as the red piece of biscuit on the blanket in our example (see Figure 7.4). The process is carried out in three steps:

a Click on the **Cloning** toolbar button .

Before   After

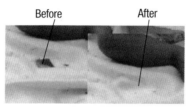

Figure 7.4

b Right-click the pointer over the area you want to use as your camouflage, such as an empty part of the white blanket.

c Using the left mouse button, gently click and drag the mouse to paint over the unwanted object or tear marks. The area you are using as camouflage (marked with an X) slowly moves out of range so you have to repeat the selection process several times to pick up exactly the right colour or texture.

5 Colour or contrast enhancement: If your picture has faded with age, or is the wrong shade, you can try the automatic contrast and colour effects. Both are available from the **Effects – Enhance Photo** menu. Automatic Colour Balance will allow you to move the pointer along a scale to emphasise the warmer or cooler colours (see Figure 7.5).

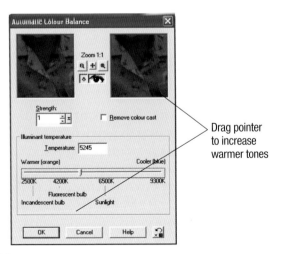

Drag pointer to increase warmer tones

Figure 7.5

Automatic Contrast Enhancement can help you increase the highlights and shadows.

6   When you have made all your changes, save the new image with a different name or in a new location, and decide whether or not to change it to a different file type (such as .jpg) that will save space but may lose a little of the detail. (For example, the above image was 86.5Kb as a JPEG and 1.18Mb as a PSP file.)

7   You can now keep the renovated photo on your computer or print it out on photographic quality printing paper.

Make life easier with the internet

The internet has revolutionised the way things are now done. It may at first seem confusing, but once you've learnt the basics there's so much you can do with it you'll begin to wonder how you got by before. Part 3 looks at just some of the many ways the internet can make your life easier.

Part 3 covers:

Find things on the web

Once you decide that you want to use your computer for searching the internet and sending messages, you must register with an Internet Service Provider (ISP). You need to provide your personal details and choose an identification – your **username** and **password** – that will safeguard your settings. The ISP:

- establishes your broadband connection or the dialling facilities that your computer will be set to dial automatically

- installs the latest browser software, such as Internet Explorer, needed for viewing web pages

- offers you an email address.

There are lots of ISPs who offer these services and all the necessary software can be installed via a CD-ROM available from shops, magazines or contacting by telephone. Load the disk into your CD-ROM drive and follow the instructions to install the software and register with the ISP. Once you have a connection, you can always change to a different ISP by registering on the new company's website once any contract has expired.

Figure 8.1

Once you have signed up with an ISP, you should be ready to double-click the Internet Explorer or ISP icon to open your browser window and connect to the world wide web (www). You may like to set the computer to remember your username and password so that connections are quick and easy, or you may have signed up for broadband and will stay connected all the time.

Web pages

Inside the browser window, a colourful web page of text and pictures should fill the screen (see Figure 8.2).

Toolbar

Address box

Web page

Figure 8.2

Working with the internet will soon become straightforward. You have several menus and toolbar buttons along the top of the browser window that will be explained later. Most useful are the **Back** and **Forward** buttons: as you visit new pages, the old ones will still be available. Click **Back** to work back through pages you have visited, or **Forward** to move on again.

Home page

Each time you open your browser, the same initial web page will be displayed. This is your home page and is usually a page of information provided by your ISP. You return here each time you click the **Home** button in your browser window. If it is not a convenient starting point for an internet session – perhaps you prefer to start by reading the news, checking what's on TV or viewing information from your housing association – you can set any page as your home page.

Type the address of your preferred web page into the Address box, over the address already showing there, and then press Enter or click the button labelled **Go**. When the page appears, open the **Tools** menu and select **Internet Options** (see Figure 8.3).

Figure 8.3

In the **Home page** section, click **Use Current** and then click **OK** to close the window (see Figure 8.4). This page will now open every time you connect to the internet or click the **Home** button in future.

Click to set
page

Confirm
settings

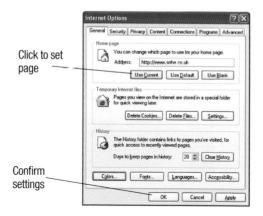

Figure 8 4

Open new pages

You can open new web pages in two ways:

1 Type the address of the page into the Address box and press Enter (or click the **Go** button) . The address is often referred to as the **URL** (Uniform Resource Locator) and will have the form www.name.co.uk (or org.uk, com, ac.uk, gov.uk, etc depending on the type of organisation it is). You may notice that at some stage the letters http:// are added automatically, but these do not need to be typed.

2 Click on the page when the pointer displays a hand. This hand appears when it is over a hyperlink that has been embedded in the web page. These links are commonly used for opening indexes or finding information that readers will want to move to within the website, and the link text usually changes colour or shows as underlined (see Figure 8.5).

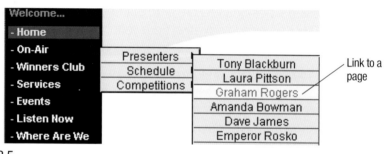

Link to a
page

Figure 8.5

Searching

There is so much information on the internet that it can be hard to locate exactly what you are looking for. In many cases, you will know which organisation can provide the information and so you will need to visit their website by typing the address in the Address box. You will see website addresses listed in magazines and newspapers or on TV, and you may already have come across some well-known ones such as **www.bbc. co.uk**, **www.ageconcern.org.uk**, **www.guardian.co.uk** or **www. inlandrevenue.gov.uk**

The problem comes when you want information that doesn't belong to a single organisation: weather reports, cricket scores, medical information, historical facts, etc. For this reason, special types of website have been set up known as search engines. Many such websites are available, including **www.google.co.uk**, **www.altavista.com**, and **www.yahoo. co.uk**

All they offer is a method for searching thousands of different websites, looking for the specific information you have asked them to find. When the list of sites appears on the page, you can click a link to any one and see if the information you are seeking is provided. In some cases, the search engines also group related websites together so that you can work through categories such as **Recreation and Leisure – Sport – Tennis – Tennis Clubs** to locate a limited number of relevant websites already catalogued for you.

When searching, you need to type a word or phrase into a box provided on screen known as the Query or Search box. These are your **keywords** and the more care you take with them, the more accurate the search results will be. For example, what if you wanted to find recipes for people who have diabetes? Here is how refining the keywords and adding symbols during a recent search on **www.google.co.uk** resulted in a shorter, more accurate and manageable list of websites to visit:

1. **Diabetes** (over 70 million results): Websites mainly covering the actual medical condition.

2. **Diabetes recipes** (268,000): Websites included many featuring books you would have to buy and still those on medical issues.

3. **Diabetes recipes** (and clicking the link to **pages from the UK**) (19,600): More helpful as sites only featured information from the UK.

4. **Diabetes recipes –books** (9,000): A more relevant and manageable list, as books were excluded by adding the minus symbol.

5 **'Diabetes recipes' –books** (546): This resulted in the shortest search list, as using quotation marks meant that 'diabetes' was not identified on the page unless it was next to the word 'recipes'.

If you are unsure of a spelling, or want to find a range of related websites, you can use the **wild card** or asterisk (*) symbol to replace parts of a word. For example, entering post* might pick up websites featuring information on postage, postcards, posters and fence posts.

One problem often encountered when searching for information and following up one of the listed sites is that the exact word or phrase may be lost in the heart of a detailed web page. If you are viewing a web page but cannot find the information easily, open the **Edit** menu and select **Find (on this Page)** (see Figure 8.6).

Figure 8.6

Type your keyword(s) into the box and click **Find Next**. A matching word should be highlighted on the page and you can keep clicking **Find Next** until the section that interests you is located (see Figure 8.7).

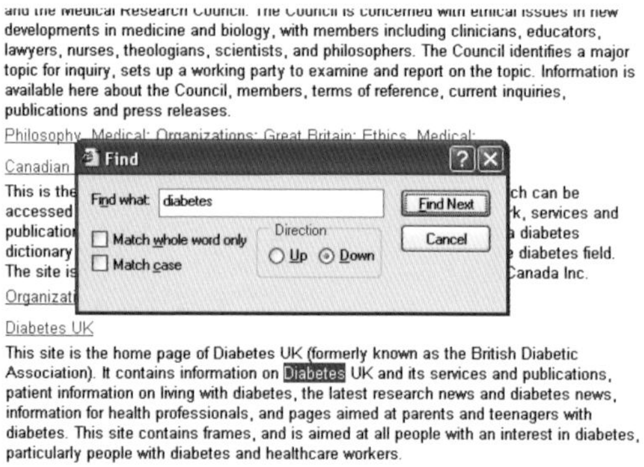

and the Medical Research Council. The Council is concerned with ethical issues in new developments in medicine and biology, with members including clinicians, educators, lawyers, nurses, theologians, scientists, and philosophers. The Council identifies a major topic for inquiry, sets up a working party to examine and report on the topic. Information is available here about the Council, members, terms of reference, current inquiries, publications and press releases.

Philosophy; Medical; Organizations; Great Britain; Ethics, Medical;

Canadian **Find** **?** **×**

This is the | Find what: diabetes | Find Next | ch can be
accessed | | k, services and
publication | ☐ Match whole word only | Direction | Cancel | a diabetes
dictionary | ☐ Match case | ○ Up ⦿ Down | | e diabetes field.
The site is | | Canada Inc.
Organizat

Diabetes UK

This site is the home page of Diabetes UK (formerly known as the British Diabetic Association). It contains information on **Diabetes** UK and its services and publications, patient information on living with diabetes, the latest research news and diabetes news, information for health professionals, and pages aimed at parents and teenagers with diabetes. This site contains frames, and is aimed at all people with an interest in diabetes, particularly people with diabetes and healthcare workers.

Figure 8.7

Example 13

Use a search engine to find a map of Age Concern offices and print a copy

Nowadays, it is very easy to print out helpful information before a journey. This can include street maps, timetables, underground maps, directions to airports and other useful data. Here is how you could locate a specific office in London.

1 With your computer connected to the internet and the browser window open, type the address of the Google search engine (www.google.co.uk) in the Address box and press the Enter key.

2 You will see several underlined labels as well as the empty Query box. In Google, there is a link to **Maps**, and as this is a very effective search facility, you should click this first (see Figure 8.8). (For different searches, you could first click **Images**, **Shopping** or **News** to limit your search to pictures, participating online shops or the latest news.)

Click for map search

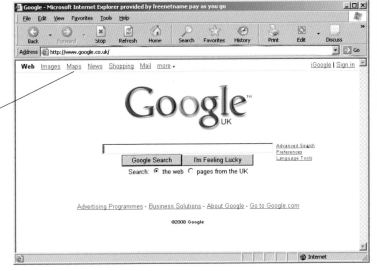

Figure 8.8

3 When the map search page opens, enter the postcode, road name or other information you are looking for and then click the **Search Maps** button.

4 A map will appear pinpointing the best match for your search, as well as offering other related locations. Each place will display a letter in a red balloon and, in a pane on the left, details of that place will be displayed.

5 Click the underlined heading in the side pane or the red balloon and full details of the location will be displayed on the map. You can even click a link to get directions to your chosen location (see Figure 8.9).

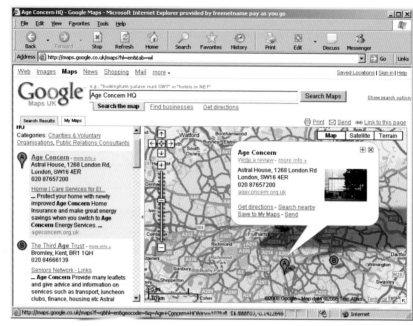

Figure 8.9

6 If you leave the Google search page at **Web**, you can explore the other map sites available.

7 There are many websites providing street maps, so type the search words 'street maps' into the Query box and press Enter to display a list of map sites. Make sure that you also click the **pages from the UK** circular (radio) button (see Figure 8.10), or type 'UK' in the Query box before searching, to limit the search to companies providing maps of the UK or parts of the UK.

Figure 8.10

8 In a few seconds, you will see a list of pages. Each one may display a brief description of its contents and the date it was last updated, and has a clickable title to take you to the website. At the top of the page you will see the number of websites located with this search (**hits**), although those at the end of the list will probably be a poor match for your keywords. Note that the links showing on the right are sponsored links, so may end up offering items you must purchase (see Figure 8.11).

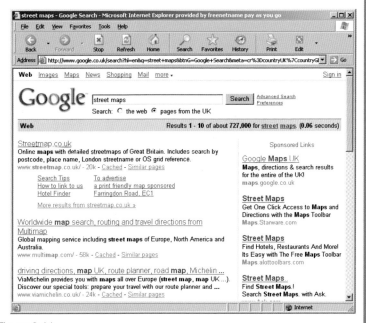

Figure 8.11

9. Click the link to the first website in the list and use the boxes on the page to enter part of the address – postcode, street name or other identifier; for example, 1268 London Road or SW16 4ER. Click the correct circular (radio) button and then click **Search** (see Figure 8.12).

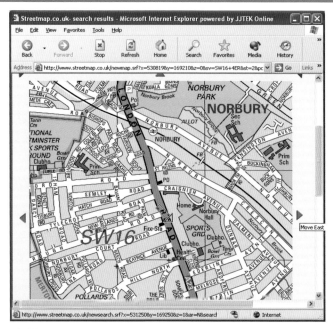

Figure 8.12

10 The map will slowly be revealed and you can drag the scroll bars up or down, click a directional arrow or change the magnification until you can see your street clearly. It is identified by an arrow in some systems and a red circle in others (see Figure 8.13).

Figure 8.13

11 If the map is not helpful, click your **Back** button to return to the search list and visit another website.

12 Once you find a satisfactory map, you can print a copy to keep. If there is a link to a printable version, click this first as it will remove the advertisements.

13 Now is the time to disconnect if you are paying for each minute online. Double-click the computer symbol on your taskbar and click the **Disconnect** button. The map will stay on screen until you close the browser window (see Figure 8.14).

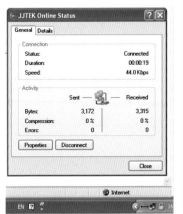

Figure 8.14

14 Printing web pages is straightforward – simply click your **Print** button to print a copy. However, a web 'page' may be longer than the usual word-processed page, so make sure that you have enough paper if you want all the information, or limit your printing to the first page. **Open File – Print** and set to print 1 page only (see Figure 8.15).

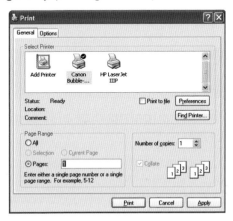

Figure 8.15

Shop online – let the high street come to you

Do you find regular shopping tiring or boring or would you simply like the luxury of having heavy items delivered straight to your door? Thousands of computer owners are now using online versions of high street stores as a replacement for at least some of their shopping trips, and more and more retailers are offering this service.

You can buy pretty much anything online, but most useful to many people is buying their groceries. All the large supermarkets provide this service now. Some will charge a fee for delivery – commonly £5 – but this may be waived if your shopping comes to more than the minimum (which may be £40, for example), or you request delivery mid-week when they are less busy. Although the websites are national, supermarket shopping is slightly different from buying from other major retailers as it involves fresh food. Instead of a national warehouse, your shopping will actually be collected in your local supermarket and brought to you by a local van driver.

Example 14

Register with a supermarket and organise delivery of your groceries

Many companies will deliver groceries, including Tesco, Waitrose, Asda and Sainsbury's. This example is based on shopping at Sainsbury's, so go to **www.sainsburys.co.uk**, but all the others work in the same way if you prefer to shop with them.

1 There is usually a link to online shopping on the main page, so click this to begin the process (see Figure 9.1).

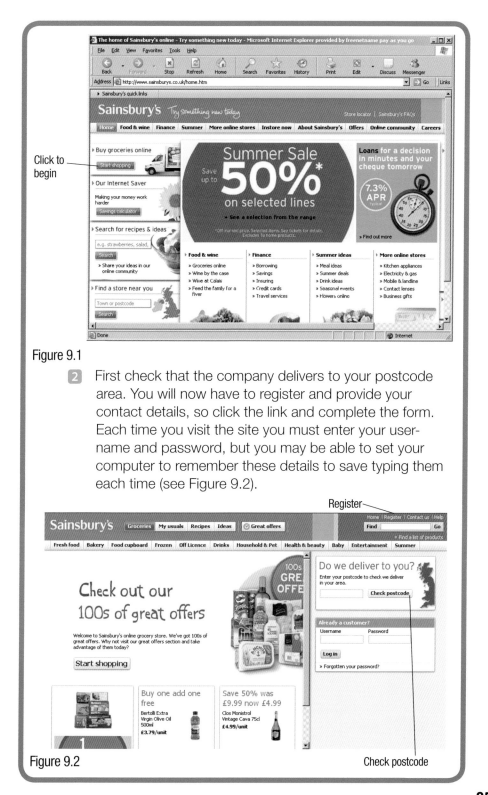

Figure 9.1

2 First check that the company delivers to your postcode
area. You will now have to register and provide your
contact details, so click the link and complete the form.
Each time you visit the site you must enter your username and password, but you may be able to set your
computer to remember these details to save typing them
each time (see Figure 9.2).

Figure 9.2

3 Most retailers offer the chance to book a delivery day and time before you start shopping, so click the link and then click on the day and time to book a slot (see Figure 9.3).

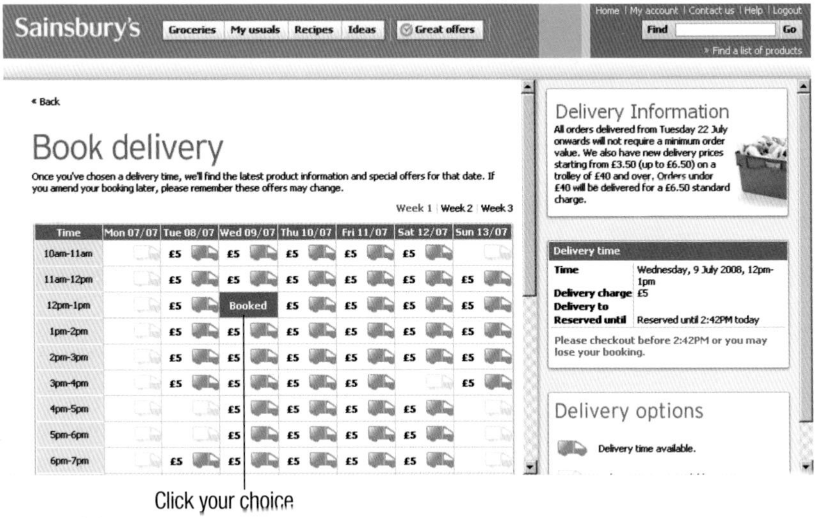

Click your choice

Figure 9.3

4 You can shop in two ways: type the name of the item in a search box and click **Find** or browse the 'aisles' (ie click a top-level category of food types and work down to your chosen items) (see Figure 9.4).

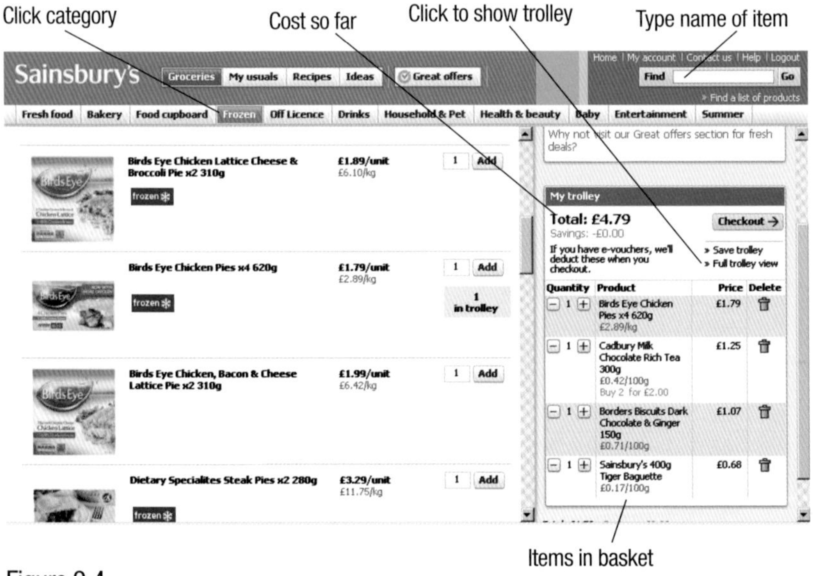

Click category   Cost so far   Click to show trolley   Type name of item

Items in basket

Figure 9.4

5 For any item you wish to buy, check it shows the correct weight or number of packs, and so on, and change these where necessary by clicking the + or - buttons. This will add or remove the item from your basket/trolley. Sometimes you can click an **Info** button to display further details. The basket will remain visible on screen or be available by clicking a labelled tab.

6 At any time, you can cancel or add items by clicking the **Trolley** tab and updating the number of items you want to order (see Figure 9.5).

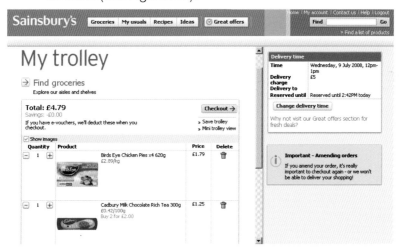

Figure 9.5

7 At the end of your shopping, click **Checkout** to pay.

8 Enter your credit or debit card details and the number on any special offer vouchers you might have been sent. You should see two signs that the website is secure for making payments: the address will begin with https:// and a padlock will be visible at the bottom of the screen (see Figure 9.6).

Figure 9.6

9 Once you have completed all the boxes, confirm your purchase and, if you want, print out a copy of your order. You should receive confirmation of the order by email and can then look forward to your groceries being delivered in a few days' time.

10 If you shop regularly, you will soon save time using the shortcuts offered. For example, you can view your last list or regular items (your usual) or jot down a list of general items on a memo pad (quick start) and choose from just these, which can make internet shopping quicker than ever.

Compare prices and save money

You can use the web to check the prices of anything from airline tickets to garden tools, mobile phones or cauliflowers. However, it takes practice and patience to end up with the very best deal. As well as using common search engines, there are websites set up specifically to compare prices. These can be very useful as a starting point but should never be relied on completely – that's because they may not sample all possible sites, they may not include hidden costs such as delivery and they may be sponsored by certain manufacturers, which can bias their results.

Example 15

Find the cheapest ergonomic kneeling chair

If you use a computer for a long period of time, and worry that you are not sitting correctly, one answer is to buy an ergonomically designed chair such as a kneeling chair.

As many shops sell a form of this chair, you can use a search engine to help you find the best buy. Remember, although we're looking for a chair in this example, you can buy pretty much anything online and you would do it in the same way as we demonstrate here.

1. When you enter the keywords into a search engine query box, three or four websites listed in the results are likely to be comparison or shopping websites, which will include names such as Kelkoo, DealTime, Nextag and Bizrate. Rather than looking up every site listed when you start your search for any item, you may think using a comparison site would save time and money.

2. Nextag, for example, lists 18 chairs (see Figure 10.1).

Figure 10.1

3 Hovering the mouse over the **Best Match** heading offers a different sort order such as from lowest to highest. (see Figure 10.2).

Figure 10.2

4 If you want to buy what appears to be the cheapest chair – which in this example is the one offered by Furnitureatwork at £38 with free delivery – click the **Go to Store** button to open up this store's website. In this example it shows the price has mysteriously increased by £2, but there is a choice of colours (see Figure 10.3).

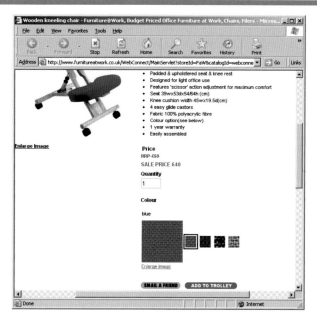

Figure 10.3

5 Click the **Add to Trolley** button to move on to the next window. After completing all personal details, you will see that the final price has jumped from the original £38 to £51.70 (see Figure 10.4). That is because a delivery charge and VAT have been added, which may not make it such a good bargain.

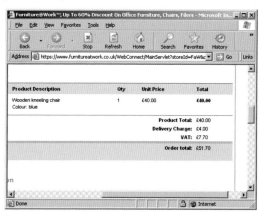

Figure 10.4

6 If you return to Nextag, you can follow links to the other stores listed. You will find that delivery costs for this type of item can range from free to over £8 and the accuracy of the original entry cannot be relied on.

7 Following the Kelkoo link may be even less helpful. Although details of postage are included on the page, one search only showed chairs from a single supplier, and all at the high end of the price range (see Figure 10.5).

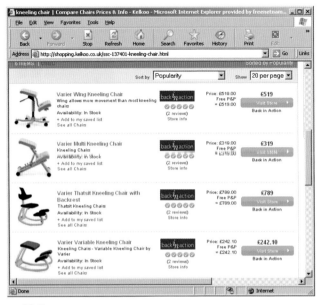

Figure 10.5

8 Bizrate was no better, as it only displayed a single chair!

9 The search producing the largest choice of chairs turned out to be the Shopping link on Google (formerly known as 'Froogle'), This resulted in over 400 possible chairs, showing their price including VAT but not shipping costs, which can only be found on the individual suppliers' websites (see Figure 10.6).

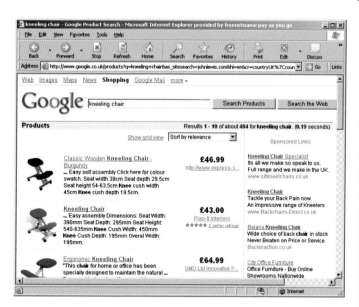

Figure 10.6

10 Not many of the major suppliers tend to be listed during comparison website searches, so one conclusion that can be drawn from this exercise is that you need to become familiar with specialist companies that have a good reputation for low-priced products such as Tesco, W H Smith (which delivers items free for collection at your local store) and Argos. Visit their websites as well as those recommended by general search engines or comparison websites before making a major purchase – they are very likely to offer good quality products and have a sensible returns policy. You could also visit an auction website such as eBay (see Chapter 16) if you are happy to buy second-hand goods or use one of eBay's associated small online stores.

Downloads for you and your computer

As well as information, games, chat rooms, tutorials and things to buy, the internet offers useful programs that will make your computer safer and easier to use. Many of these programs are available free and you can save them onto your computer through a process known as *downloading*.

In particular, you may want to download:

- Drivers: this is software that enables you to use items such as graphics cards, printers and scanners. Although you will have installed the original software when you first bought your new piece of equipment, the manufacturers are continually making improvements so that now and again it is a good idea to move up to newer versions, to make sure you run the equipment as efficiently as possible. Drivers are free to download from the manufacturers' own websites. There are 'generic' versions available that work with a range of similar equipment, but the ideal is to download programs specifically aimed at your make and model. If you can, keep a note of all the details when you first buy hardware items, so you will have these to hand when required.

- Utilities: there are a range of programs available that make life easier. For example they can:

  - help clean up your computer (eg Easy Remover Pro)

  - allow you to read certain types of file (eg Adobe Acrobat Reader)

  - make downloading faster (eg Fresh Download)

  - work as an alternative browser to Internet Explorer (eg Mozilla)

  - prevent annoying pop-up adverts appearing every few minutes (eg Pop-Up Stopper).

- Anti-virus software: Some people try to spread programs known as viruses over the internet that cause computers to crash or send out thousands of meaningless emails. For home users, they are often more of a nuisance than anything else, but you will want to prevent them gaining access to your machine. The software needed will check for viruses whenever you start your computer, receive emails or spend time on the internet. Commonly bought programs are produced by Norton and McAfee, but you can also find free software. As new viruses are produced on a regular basis, you will find that you need to update the software regularly. Most anti-virus programs include a button to click labelled **Update** that will automatically connect you to the software producer's website and download and install the latest version on your computer.

Example 16

Download the virus checker AVG and use it to scan your computer

A good quality, free program for checking for viruses is produced by Grisoft. This is called AVG and can be located at Grisoft's website (**free.grisoft.com**).

1 On the page, click the link to the free version (see Figure 11.1).

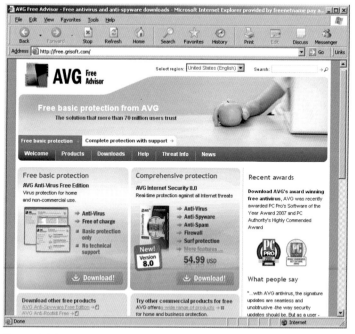

Figure 11.1

95

2 You may need to work through several screens before you can actually start downloading, so make sure you do not select a version that requires payment.

3 Click the **Download** button to start the process (see Figure 11.2).

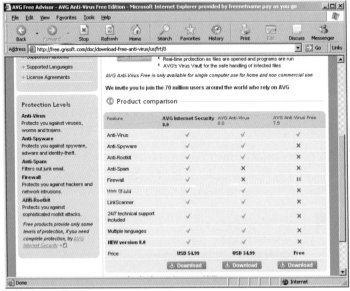

Figure 11.2

Figure 11.3

4 You may have to click another button or the download may start automatically (see Figure 11.3). When the security warning appears, choose **Save** and decide where you want to save the program to, as you will need to locate it to install it properly once it is has downloaded to your computer (see Figure 11.4). One option is to save it to your desktop, where it will be clearly visible.

Figure 11.4

5 Once the process starts, you will see a window showing the progress of the download and how long it will take. You can carry out other tasks on your computer, but must not disconnect from the internet until you reach the end of the process. To help remind you that the process is complete, click in the box to specify that the window closes once download is complete (see Figure 11.5).

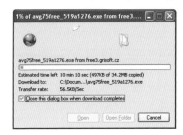

Figure 11.5

6 The file will be visible on your desktop, if saved there (see Figure 11.6), or you will need to find it on your computer. It will probably be in a newly labelled subfolder within your programs folder.

Figure 11.6

7 Open and click **Run** to start the setup process (see Figure 11.7).

Figure 11.7

8 You can now use the Wizard to help you (see Figure 11.8).

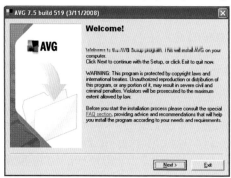

Figure 11.8

9 When setup is complete, you may need to restart your computer so that all the necessary settings can be confirmed. You can then use the program to check your computer or to download the latest updates over the internet.

The colourful icon for the anti-virus program will be added to your taskbar and the software will check your computer every time you start a new session or receive emails. Open the Control Centre to check for updates or click **Test Centre** to carry out a scan at any time (see Figure 11.9).

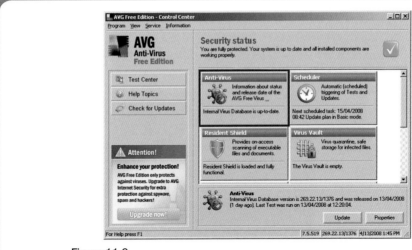

Figure 11.9

Example 17

Work with PDF files

One type of file commonly found on the internet is a **PDF**. This stands for Portable Document Format and is a popular way for documents to be distributed on the web, as they retain all their formatting and layout. Common documents of this type include manuals, official reports and syllabuses.

When searching the web, you may be offered information in PDF format, with an alternative option to view it as an HTML file. Here, the layout will be far less clear (see Figure 11.10).

Figure 11.10

When you find a PDF on a website, it will display a recognisable red symbol:

This shows that you need to have the Adobe Acrobat Reader installed on your computer before you can open and read it fully. Go to www.adobe.com. to download a free version (see Figure 11.11).

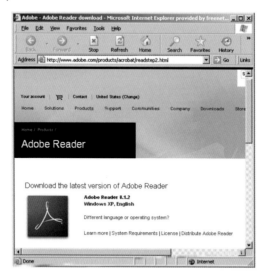

Figure 11.11

1 To view a PDF file, you can open and read it by clicking the link on a web page in the normal way. To keep it for the future, right-click, select **Save Target As** and store it in a suitable folder. You then don't need to wait for it to open on screen before saving.

2 Once you have Adobe Reader on your computer, it will open the file automatically. You will see the first page of the document in the Adobe window (see Figure 11.12):

   a At the top are several boxes and buttons. These let you check the number of pages and you can click the arrows to move backwards or forwards; increase or decrease magnification; save or print the document and display it as continuous or separate pages.

b Down the side of the page are extra options: Pages lets you see all the pages as thumbnails; Binoculars lets you carry out a search for specific words; the green circle is a link to Help and the paperclip to view any attachments in a separate window.

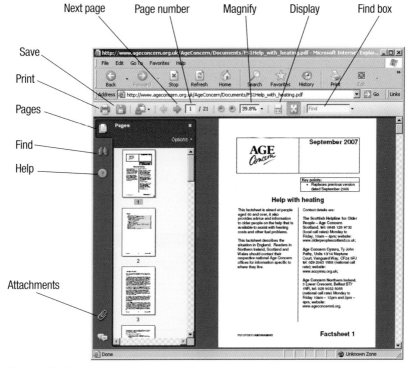

Figure 11.12

3 There are various ways to move through a PDF document:

a Click the Next or Previous page arrows above the document.

b Click a thumbnail in the left-hand pane.

c Press the Page Up or Page Down keys.

d Scroll with the mouse.

e Enter a specific page number into the box and press Enter to go to that page.

4 You may want to copy items from a PDF file to add them to other documents. Do this in the latest version of Adobe by selecting the text or image in the normal way with the mouse and then right-clicking the mouse button. Select **Copy** from the menu and then paste the item into your new document. (With older versions, you needed to click the appropriate text or image selection tool first.)

5 To search a PDF for the next mention of a specific word or phrase, type it in the Find box and click the drop-down arrow next to the box. Click the **Find Next** option and then click the pages that will appear to keep checking each single entry in turn.

6 To search for all entries, either click the **Binoculars** link and enter the text into the box or use the Find box to open the search pane. After clicking the **Search** button, all matching entries will be listed in the box (see Figure 11.13).

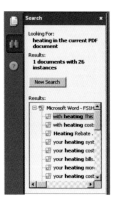

Figure 11.13

Keep in touch with emails and attachments

No computer user should be without an email address. You can then send messages and files around the world in just a few seconds, at minimum cost. During the process of registering with an ISP for dial-up or broadband connections to view the world wide web, you will have created an email address. Some ISPs, such as AOL, provide their own email software but in most cases you can use a program already installed on your computer, such as Outlook Express .

Email address

Your address will be made up of a username or ID, @ and then the name of your ISP, for example:

> Username@compuserve.com

or

> Username@btinternet.co.uk

The username is normally a combination of your initials or first name and surname, perhaps with the addition of a number, and is chosen by you during the registration process. As someone else may already have chosen your preferred username, have several others ready in case you need to suggest a suitable alternative.

Working with Outlook Express

Open Outlook Express by double-clicking the icon . You will see the page shown in Figure 12.4, but you can set the system to start in your mailbox each time you open it in future. If you are not on broadband and your computer tries to connect to the internet when you open Outlook Express, click the **Work offline** button. It will save your telephone bill if you only connect when you want to send or receive emails.

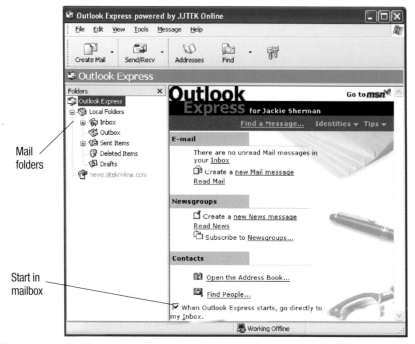

Mail folders

Start in mailbox

Figure 12.4

Folders

On the left you can see the folders in which messages will be stored. Click any one to see its contents on the right. The folders are:

- Inbox: all new messages arrive here and the number of unread messages is shown in brackets next to the folder name. Double-click any message to read it in its own window.

- Outbox: a temporary storage folder where messages wait until you connect to the internet and send them.

- Sent Items: copies of all messages that have been sent are stored here.

- Drafts: if you want to continue working on a message, save it here temporarily.

- Deleted Items: messages you don't want to keep are stored here until you choose to empty this folder.

Creating a message

Click the **Create Mail** button 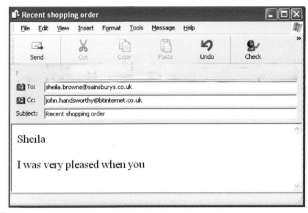 · and complete the boxes in the new message window that opens (see Figure 12.5):

- **To:** the full email address of anyone you are writing to.

- **Cc:** the full email address of anyone who should receive a copy of your message, including any attachments.

- **Subject:** a summary of the contents of your message.

Figure 12.5

Type your message in the main window and then decide which of the following actions is appropriate:

- Click the **Send** button to move your message to the Outbox and start the dial-up process to connect to the internet. If you are online, the message will be sent straightaway.

- **File – Send Later** will place the message in your Outbox but not start connecting. You can write several more messages and send them all at the same time when you have finished.

- **File – Save** will place the message in your Drafts folder so that you can continue working on it at a later date.

If you previously delayed sending messages but you are now ready to do so, click the **Send/Receive** button in the main window · to connect to the internet and send all the messages in your Outbox. You will also receive any messages that have been sent to you in the meantime.

105

Web-based email

If you don't have your own computer or software such as Outlook Express, but want to send and receive emails using public computers in libraries or colleges, you can register for a free web address at websites such as **www.yahoo.co.uk**, **www.hotmail.com** or **www.easypeasy.com**. Once registered, you can log on from any computer whenever you access the internet and use your message system online.

To register, you will need to provide both a username and a secret password known only to you. It is very important that you remember the exact wording (and case) of your username and password as you will need to type them each time you want to use the service.

Example 18

Register for a web-based email address

Web-based email systems work in a similar way, so here is how to register with easypeasy.

1. Type in www.easypeasy.com in the Address box in your browser and then press Enter or click **Go**.

2. Click the free email link (see Figure 12.1).

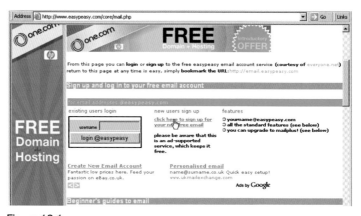

Figure 12.1

3 Select the free account to register. You will be presented with an online form and must complete all the boxes (see Figure 12.2).

| Address | http://easypeasy.mail.everyone.net/email/scripts/collectRegistrationInfo.pl | ▼ | 🔁 Go | Links |

Create New easypeasy Account

All information is required unless noted otherwise.   **Step 1 of 2**

User Name:	Pete @easypeasy.com	Your user name must contain at least 3 characters.
Password:	••••••••	Your password must contain at least 6 characters.
Re-enter Password:	••••••••	
Password Question:	mother's maiden name	You will need to know your Password Answer to obtain a new password.
Password Answer:	Smith	
First Name:	Peter	Your privacy is important. Please read the Privacy Policy on the bottom of this page to learn how your privacy is protected.
Last Name:		
Address:		

| Done | | 🌐 Internet |

Figure 12.2

The password will display as a series of asterisks (***) or dots (•••) so that no one standing nearby can see what you have typed. The secret question is a prompt and it is up to you what you put in the question and answer boxes. If you forget your password, being able to type the correct answer to the question may mean you are still allowed access to your mail.

4 After completing the form and submitting it, you will see that you have been registered. You can now sign in each time you want to use the service by completing the username and password boxes (see Figure 12.3).

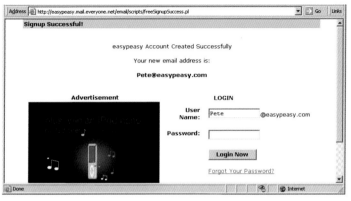

| Address | http://easypeasy.mail.everyone.net/email/scripts/freeSignupSuccess.pl | ▼ | 🔁 Go | Links |

Signup Successful!

easypeasy Account Created Successfully

Your new email address is:

Pete@easypeasy.com

Advertisement   **LOGIN**

User Name: Pete   @easypeasy.com

Password:

Login Now

Forgot Your Password?

| Done | | 🌐 Internet |

Figure 12.3

Example 19

Send a picture as an email attachment

If you took a picture of your pet as described in Example 9, you might like to follow these instructions to send it to a friend or relative by email. You can use exactly the same process to send someone a copy of a spreadsheet, presentation or text document.

1 Write your message and then click the **Attach** button showing a paperclip (see Figure 12.6), or open the **Insert** menu and select **File Attachment**.

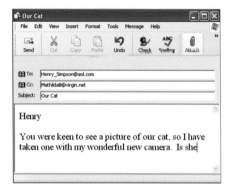

Figure 12.6

2 You will open your computer folders. Browse through the files on your computer and when you find the file you want to send, select it and then click the **Attach** button (see Figure 12.7).

Figure 12.7

3 Back in your message, you will see the file in a new **Attach** box (see Figure 12.8).

Henry

Figure 12.8

You can repeat the process to add further files to the message, and then send it as normal.

4 If the file you want to send is very large, it is a good idea to compress it first, so that it takes up less space. Windows XP compresses files by a process known as *zipping*. To zip a file, first locate the file by opening My Computer and then opening the folders inside until you can see the image file name. Right-click the name and select **Send To – Compressed (zipped) Folder** (see Figure 12.9).

Figure 12.9

A new folder displaying a zip appears at the end of the list of files Rose1. It has the same name as the image file and contains the file in a compressed format. This folder can be attached to an email in exactly the same way as a normal file.

As long as your recipient has Windows XP or a program that works with zipped files, such as WinZip, they can double-click the file to open it again.

5 If you receive a message containing an attachment, it will display a paperclip when it first arrives in your Inbox 🔋 📎.

6 The file will be displayed in the Attach box when you open the message fully, so double-click to open it. You will be offered the option to save the file to disk rather than open it directly, as it may contain viruses (see Figure 12.10). This will enable you to run your virus checker to make sure it is safe.

Figure 12.10

Have fun

One of the things most people love about their computer is that it's not only incredibly useful but it can also be fantastic fun! It's great for hobbies, meeting new people, listening to your favourite music, playing games and much more besides. Part 4 looks at just a few of the many things you can do to have fun using your computer.

Part 4 covers:

Meet others on the web

As well as emails that are sent to people in the form of electronic 'letters', there are other ways to communicate via the internet. The two most common are: **chat rooms**, which are equivalent to real-time conversations; and **social networks**, **forums** or **message boards**, which can be thought of as a cross between emailing a large group of strangers and pinning up notices on a notice board. If you want to communicate specifically with older people, Age Concern has forums on its main website and a chat room named the Baby Boomer Bistro.

For all these systems, you are required to register and provide basic details about yourself. You must also agree to rules governing such things as the language you use, so that no one is upset by what takes place. Some systems have a moderator who keeps an eye on proceedings, but this is not always the case.

Much is heard about the dangers of chat rooms and social networks such as Facebook, simply because no one knows the true identity of anyone using them. Instead, you are asked to choose a nickname by which you will be known. For this reason, you should take great care and never reveal too much personal information about yourself.

Chat rooms

When you click a link to a chat room you are online at the same time as everyone else taking part in the discussion. (If no one else appears, there is nothing much you can do except try again another day.) Once you have made the link, your nickname will be revealed to the other users and you can join in the conversation whenever you like by typing your comments in a small box below the screen and then pressing Enter. Your text will soon appear on a new line. You can exit the room at any time.

One slightly disconcerting aspect of chat rooms is that there is always a small delay between typing and seeing your words on screen, so you may find yourself replying to a topic that has moved on!

Forums, social networks and message boards

Forums, social networks and message boards do not require you to be present at any particular time. When you read a message that you want to reply to, click the **Reply** button, type your comments and then send them in. Writing replies in this way on the web is known as **posting** and next time you visit the forum you will see your reply and perhaps others that have been added in the meantime. Messages are normally left on the board for days or months, and in many cases contain helpful advice and tips from experts on the topic of the forum. Examples of forums on the Age Concern website include books, gardening and IT.

Example 20

Join in a Baby Boomer Bistro chat room

1 Go to the website at **www.babyboomerbistro.org.uk** or **www.ageconcern.org/discuss/chat**.

2 You will need to register, so click the link (see Figure 13.1) and complete the details (see Figure 13.2). If you make any mistakes, you will be directed back to complete those particular boxes again.

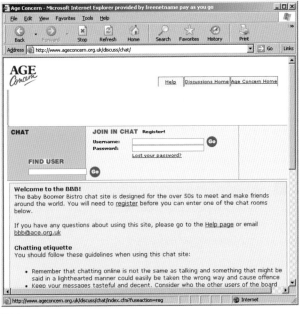

Figure 13.1

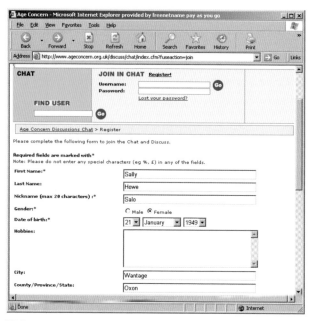

Figure 13.2

3 Once registered, your password is sent to the email address you provided and you can log in by typing your chat nickname and password into the appropriate boxes. This is the process you must repeat every time you want to chat in the future.

4 Once inside the website, you will see that there are several 'rooms' to visit. Different people will get together in these, perhaps establishing a certain style of conversation or discussing particular topics, and so it is a good idea to visit each one and watch the current conversation unfold for a while.

5 As anyone joining a room is identified to the others, you will probably be welcomed. Type your reply in the box under the window and press Enter to add it to the conversation (see Figure 13.3).

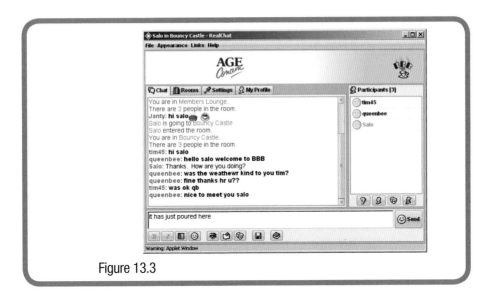

Figure 13.3

Example 21

Add comments to an Age Concern forum

1 Visit the main website by entering **www.ageconcern.org. uk** in your browser address box. On the page, click the **Staying active** link to find discussions (see Figure 13.4).

Figure 13.4

2 Once again, you must first register and choose an appropriate nickname so that you are able to log in. Although you can read the messages without doing so, you will not be able to reply or start any new discussions.

3 Look at the subjects listed on the page and click any tab to view them in more detail (see Figure 13.5).

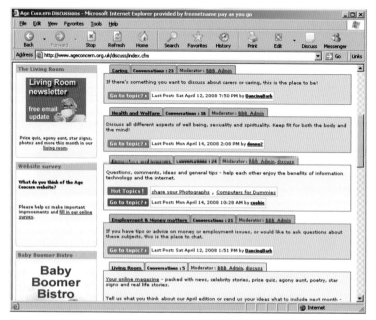

Figure 13.5

4 You will see how many messages each topic has attracted so far, and can click the name to view these. They are arranged by date and you can read through them all or click any page number (see Figure 13.6).

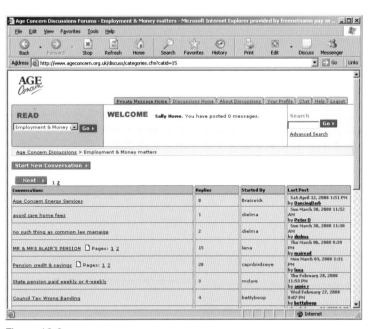

Figure 13.6

5 If you see a comment to which you would like to reply, or you have a question to ask, click the **Post Your Reply** button and then type in your message in the box provided, before submitting it for publication on the forum (see Figure 13.7).

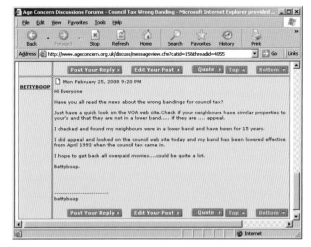

Figure 13.7

Radio online or on the move

Do you fancy listening to digital broadcasts without buying a new radio; would you like to hear programmes you missed the first time round; have you wondered what type of programmes people listen to in America or Australia; or would you enjoy music or local news at odd times of the day or night? If so, you can now tune in online. So many people are doing this that alongside well-known services such as BBC Radio 4 (see Figure 14.1) or the World Service, there are many internet-only radio stations catering for a wide range of tastes.

Figure 14.1

Podcasts

If you have an MP3 player such as the Apple iPod, you can now also listen to syndicated material created specially as audio files in a form known as **podcasts** (or view videos as **vodcasts**). These can be played both on portable media players, so you can take them with you wherever you go, or simply on your computer at home. If you subscribe to a podcast, future episodes will be sent to your computer automatically – and subscriptions are currently free of any charges.

Podcasts use Really Simple Syndication (RSS) technology and publishers of the material send out a file known as an RSS feed linked to the MP3 files. To listen to podcasts, you need software such as iTunes, Doppler or Juice (known as podcast aggregators) that can read these feeds (see Figure 14.2). Once installed, you open the program and simply click the podcast subscription link on any web page to receive future programmes without having to visit the actual website again.

Figure 14.2

Your Windows XP machine should have a sound card and the necessary software, in the form of Windows Media Player, to listen to most of the radio output. However, some services may require different software, such as RealPlayer or RealOnePlayer, which is available free to download from websites such as the BBC at **www. bbc.co.uk/radio/help/faq/download_and_install_realplayer. shtml** (see Figure 14.3).

119

Figure 14.3

Finding radio websites

You may know some sites that you want to visit, such as the BBC, Radio Now (**www.radio-now.co.uk**) or Classic Gold (**www.mygoldmusic. co.uk**), but your player offers a good range of stations as a starting point.

Click the Media toolbar button on the taskbar to open the player.

Select Media Guide from the menu and then click the **Go to Radio** link to see some choices, or **Radio Tuner** to display a list of featured stations (see Figures 14.4 and 14.5).

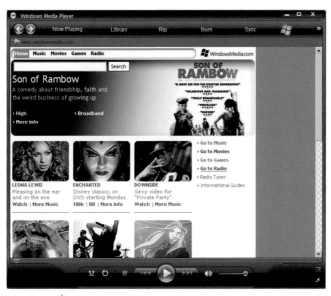

Figure 14.4

Figure 14.5

You will display a list of stations including the BBC World Service that you can listen to. Click any station name to find further details and a **Play** button, or to go to the station's website (see Figure 14.6).

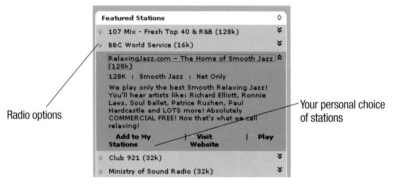

Figure 14.6

Each website is organised differently, but there should be links to different programmes or types of music. Navigate through the menus and click any link that says **Listen** or **Play Now** (see Figures 14.7a and 14.7b).

Figure 14.7a

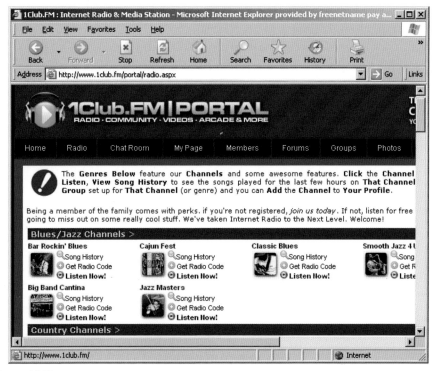

Figure 14.7b

Even if you launch Media Player in fullscreen mode, you can always minimise the window and continue working on your computer and the station will play in the background.

Example 22

Bookmark favourite radio website addresses

Bookmarking is the term used for adding website links to a folder on your computer so that you can visit the sites again very quickly. The folder holding bookmarked sites is labelled Favorites in Internet Explorer and is accessed by opening the browser. Any web page can be linked in this way, and your bookmarked pages ('favourites') can be grouped and organised in the same way that you organise your computer files and folders. Although the following example shows how to bookmark internet radio sites, the same technique can be used for any websites you visit frequently.

123

Once you find a radio station offering a choice of programmes or music of special interest, you will want to keep the website address handy. Although recently listened to stations will be added to the recently played list, and you can click a link labelled **Add to My Stations** so they can be found again easily, you may want to group particular types of station and otherwise manage the links, or visit the website without opening the Media Player. One way is to add stations to your Favorites folder.

1. With the web page open in your browser window, click the **Favorites** button or select it from the menu bar. This displays a list of folders that have already been created (see Figure 14.8).

Figure 14.8

2. Click the **Add** button to add your new radio website to the list (you may need to click **Create in** to view the list of folders) (see Figure 14.9):

   a. Change the linked page name, if necessary.

   b. Select an appropriate folder in which to store the link, or click **New Folder** and create a new one.

   c. Click **OK** when the folder is selected in the list and the link will be stored inside.

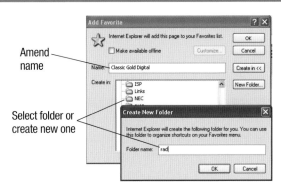

Amend name

Select folder or create new one

Figure 14.9

3 If you visit other radio websites you want to link to, click **Favorites – Add** and then click your new radio folder name in the list before clicking **OK**. If you first select this parent folder and then click **New Folder**, you can subdivide it so that certain web page links are grouped together.

4 To visit any website another day, open the **Favorites** menu, click the named folder and select the target website (see Figure 14.10). When you click it with your mouse, it will open on screen.

Figure 14.10

5 To make changes to the contents of your favourite folders, right-click the web address on screen and select an option or drag it to a new folder (see Figure 14.11). You can also open the **Favorites** menu and click **Organize**. You can then delete links, move them to different folders or rename them.

Figure 14.11

Online games

If you like playing certain games such as cribbage, scrabble or chess, type the name into a search engine query box to find out where they can be downloaded or played online. However, if you are not dedicated to a specific game, visit one of the many websites – such as **www. realarcade.com**, **games.yahoo.com** or **www.coffeebreakarcade. com/games/** – that offer the chance to play a wide range of games including fantasy, puzzle, card or board games. Many sites also provide chat room facilities so that you see the nicknames of other people playing and can chat to them during your games session.

Example 23

Play a game of Word Whomp online

This game is similar to another you will find on many game websites called Text Twist. It requires you to make words from a limited number of letters, playing against the clock, and you can ask the computer to reorder the letters to help you think of new words. Click the letters to add them to the grid, and click Enter to submit the word. As you progress, you work up to harder levels.

1 One gaming website that offers the chance to play this game is **www.pogo.com**, so visit the site and register with your basic details and a nickname for others to use. You will see details of its range of games on the main home page (see Figure 15.1).

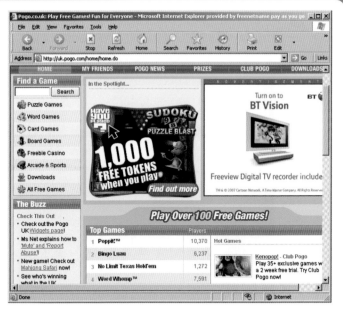

Figure 15.1

2 Click any category of game and see how many people are playing. Click any link to sign in or play the game as a guest.

3 If the game is new to you, find out how to play by reading the rules before you start (see Figure 15.2).

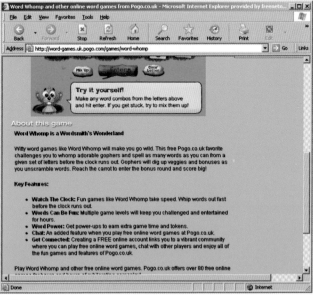

Figure 15.2

4 When you are ready, start playing (see Figure 15.3). If you have registered, you can chat to other people playing the game at the same time.

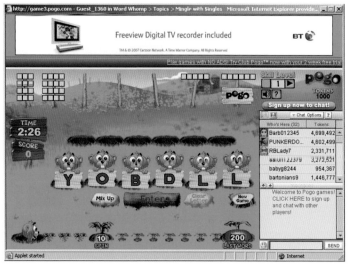

Figure 15.3

Online auctions – buying and selling

Nowadays, the pleasure and excitement of visiting a car boot sale has been superseded by taking part in an internet auction. There are several auction websites, but the most famous by far is **www.eBay.co.uk**. It works on the principle that one person's rubbish is another's treasure, and you can buy anything from antiques to clothes, furniture or jewellery.

However, people will usually only buy from sellers who have received positive feedback about their activities. Once a seller is given negative feedback, perhaps because the goods didn't turn up or were not as described, it will be hard for them to regain the confidence of other customers. It is therefore reasonably safe to take part, as long as you use your common sense:

- Don't respond to emails you receive offering something similar after you lose an item in an auction on eBay – you will not have eBay's protection.

- Set up an international payment system, for example using PayPal (see page 135), and use a credit card wherever possible, so that you are more likely to receive compensation if your goods are not supplied.

- No site can ever be 100% safe, so take great care if purchasing expensive items – losing £10 may be bearable but losing £1,000 may not.

- Some people set up fake websites that look as if they are genuine auctions – make sure the appropriate questions and screens are offered and, if you are unhappy about anything, don't continue with a purchase but send details to eBay so that it can investigate the site.

Example 24

Buy a second-hand audio CD on eBay

Goods on eBay are filed under categories; so many people search a specific category rather than the whole site to look for specific items. This is important when it comes to selling your goods, as you will have more viewings for your items in the correct category, but also makes it easier to buy. Just find the most appropriate category and start searching from here.

1 Go to the eBay website and either type a keyword in the Search box (such as a singer or band name), or first click the **Music** category in the left-hand column to search within this (see Figure 16.1).

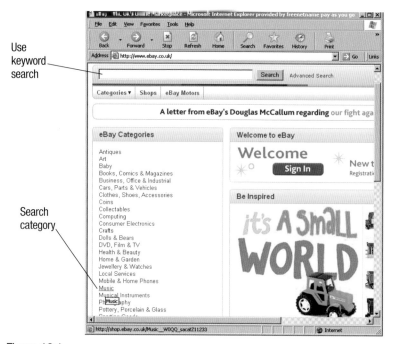

Use keyword search

Search category

Figure 16.1

2 After clicking the **Search** button or a link such as **See all items** or **CDs**, a list of all related items currently for sale appears on the screen. Some have pictures of the object and all display the price. They either show when they were listed or, if you click the **Time Listed** button, how long you have left to bid. Most items are on sale for seven or ten days (see Figure 16.2).

Figure 16.2

3 To see further details of any items of interest, click the blue, underlined title. You will find details of the seller, a fuller description of the item, postage costs and how many people have already bid for it. You can even send an email to the seller if you have a question about the item (see Figure 16.3).

Date and time
auction ends

Seller

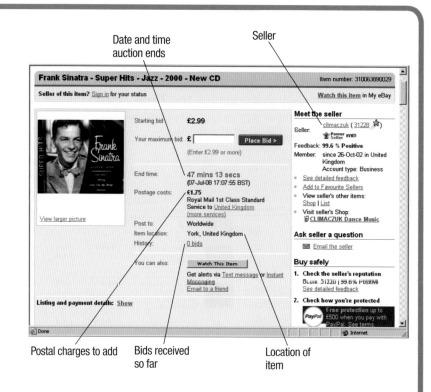

Postal charges to add

Bids received
so far

Location of
item

Figure 16.3

Figure 16.4

4 When you find an item you want to buy, click the **Place Bid** button on the details page. If you don't want to wait for the end of the auction and you are offered an acceptable price at which you can buy straightaway, click the **Buy It Now** button (see Figure 16.4). Not all items have this option, but it can save the disappointment of losing out to someone who puts in a higher bid than you.

Sometimes you may even be offered the chance to make an offer below the Buy It Now price, which could well be accepted.

5   If you want to buy anything, you have to be registered on the website. Click the register link and complete the online form. You *must* have a valid email address, as you will be sent messages telling you the state of your bid and, at the end of the auction, whether you have won and how to pay.

6   All eBay users have an ID so that their details are not revealed on screen to the general public and to allow access to their own account (see Figure 16.5).

Figure 16.5

7   Bidding involves entering the maximum price you are prepared to pay. The website will enter the lowest possible bid and, as others join in, will continue to bid on your behalf automatically over the next hours or days up to your maximum or until the auction ends (see Figure 16.6). You will either win the item or lose it to someone who enters a price higher than your maximum.

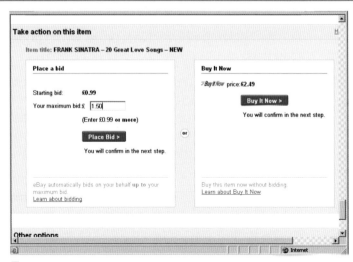

Figure 16.6

8 Once you have agreed the bid, you will see a confirmation that you are currently the highest bidder and you will receive an email to this effect (see Figure 16.7).

Figure 16.7

9 Near the end of the auction, go online if you want to watch the prices change – you need to click your **Refresh** button 🔄 to see the latest entries. If no one outbids you, you will be notified that you have won and will need to pay on the website (see Figure 16.8). A link to the page for payment and feedback will be included in your final email as well as on the site.

Figure 16.8

10 If you have not registered with PayPal, now is a good time to do so. Click the link to sign up and select the appropriate type of account before completing the email and credit card details. If you want to sell goods on a regular basis, you may prefer a business account that allows you to accept credit card payments.

You will need to choose a password to allow you to access your account each time you buy or if you want to change any details (see Figure 16.9). The money for any goods you buy will now be taken from your bank by PayPal and sent to the seller's bank without the need for you to type in your credit card details again.

Figure 16.9

11 Although it is not strictly necessary, some people contact the seller directly, to provide further details for the delivery of their goods.

Example 25

Sell an old video on eBay

1 Click the **Sell** link on the opening screen and log in with your username and password. You must be registered with eBay before you can sell anything. Check the **Quick Sell** option then click the **Start selling** button.

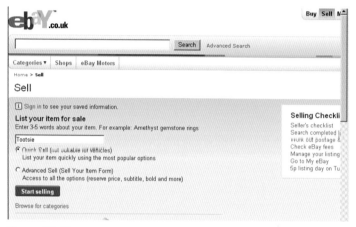

Figure 16.10

2 Type in the details of your item in the box. Either click **Browse** and then a name in the list or click the **Find a category** button for a list of suggested groupings.

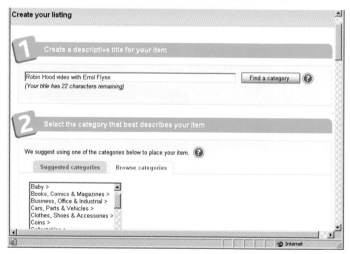

Figure 16.11

3　Most items on eBay need to be displayed visually to attract buyers, so take a picture of your object with a digital camera and add this to the page by clicking **Add a photo (Free)** then finding the picture file stored on your computer. Videos, records and DVDs, for example, would simply need a copy of the box cover or sleeve. For certain items, providing different views or close-ups will be important, so pay the few pence to add further pictures if necessary.

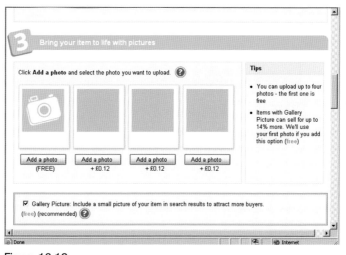

Figure 16.12

4　The section number 4 shown in Figure 16.13 is the place to describe your item in detail. The title will appear in blue, underlined text on the main page when people search, so make sure it is clear what is being sold. Some sections are included in the basic price, but you can pay for extra features, such as a subtitle if you want to make your advertisement stand out even more.

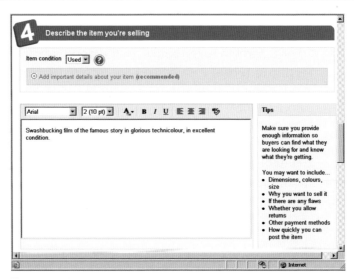

Figure 16.13

5 Start the bidding at a low figure to get the ball rolling. If you would be unhappy letting your item go for less than a specific price, you need to click the link at the bottom of the page to go to the **Sell your item** form. Here there are various options including the chance to set a **Reserve price**. Regular eBay members can fix a **Buy It Now** price if they want to offer this facility as well.

Auctions normally run for seven or ten days, and it is important to think about the timing as it will end at the same time of day as it started. If selling in the UK only, you should make sure that people will be home from work when the last frantic minutes of bidding take place.

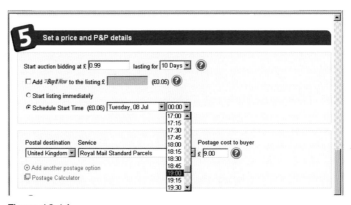

Figure 16.14

6 Set the postage costs that your buyer must add, unless you are offering free postage as part of the deal or you want to discuss delivery with the buyer after the auction.

7 Decide on the payment methods you will accept, bearing in mind that PayPal (see page 135) is the safest but there is a handling fee.

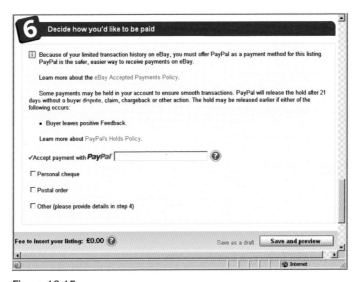

6 Decide how you'd like to be paid

[i] Because of your limited transaction history on eBay, you must offer PayPal as a payment method for this listing. PayPal is the safer, easier way to receive payments on eBay.

Learn more about the eBay Accepted Payments Policy.

Some payments may be held in your account to ensure smooth transactions. PayPal will release the hold after 21 days without a buyer dispute, claim, chargeback or other action. The hold may be released earlier if either of the following occurs:

• Buyer leaves positive Feedback.

Learn more about PayPal's Holds Policy.

✓Accept payment with **PayPal**

☐ Personal cheque

☐ Postal order

☐ Other (please provide details in step 4)

Fee to insert your listing: **£0.00**   Save as a draft   **Save and preview**

Figure 16.15

8 At the bottom of the screen click **Save and preview** to check how your listing appears and what you have to pay. If you are happy with your entry, click **Place listing**. If there are any errors or omissions, you will only be able to make changes at a later date if the bidding hasn't started or you haven't received any bids.

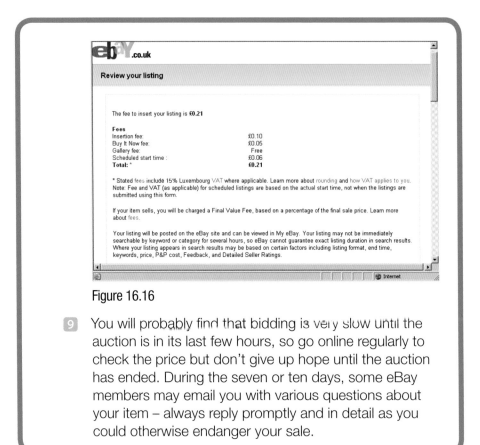

Figure 16.16

9 You will probably find that bidding is very slow until the auction is in its last few hours, so go online regularly to check the price but don't give up hope until the auction has ended. During the seven or ten days, some eBay members may email you with various questions about your item – always reply promptly and in detail as you could otherwise endanger your sale.

Learn from a CD-ROM

A brief look at the shelves of many local shops will reveal a treasure trove of CD-ROMs that you can buy for as little as £4.99. They will teach you anything from how to type to making a will, using voice recognition software, designing a garden, selecting wine, finding the best pub or creating cartoons. They will also provide hours of entertainment in the form of computerised sports, fantasy, board or card games.

Before buying a CD-ROM, check the minimum requirements printed on the back of the case or in the accompanying booklet. You will be told the best version for your PC, the memory (RAM), sound card, processor speed and monitor settings that are necessary to run the program effectively. Don't be too worried if you have a reasonably modern machine and only want to run a simple program, but some of the advanced games may not run without the very latest sound and graphics cards.

To find out more about your machine, right-click the **My Computer** icon on the desktop and select **Properties**. You will find the Windows version, RAM and processor speed of your machine (see Figure 17.1).

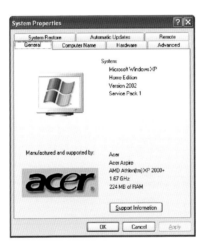

Figure 17.1

Example 26

Install and use a food encyclopaedia CD-ROM

Although you may have hundreds of recipe books, a food CD can be very helpful in planning meals. Not only can you create a quick list of many dishes that use the ingredients you happen to have in the fridge, you can also find out about their vitamin or mineral content and how to prepare unusual foods.

1 Insert the disk in your CD-ROM drive and wait for it to start automatically. If nothing happens after a few minutes, go to **Start** – **Run** and then click **Browse** (see Figure 17.2).

Figure 17.2

2 Locate the D:\ drive from the drop-down list in the **Look in:** box and then open the file labelled *Install* or *Setup* (see Figure 17.3). A file ending .exe will appear in the **Run** box and you must click **OK** to start the process.

Figure 17.3

3 The first window for the installation process appears and you can use the Wizard to install the program on your computer by clicking **Next** each time (see Figure 17.4).

Unless you are sure you want to change these, accept the locations and names that are selected automatically.

Figure 17.4

4 The files needed to run the program will be copied onto your computer (see Figure 17.5).

Figure 17.5

5 Whenever it appears, read and then click to accept the licence agreement (see Figure 17.6).

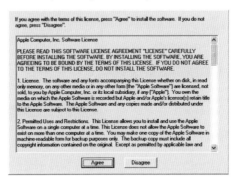

Figure 17.6

6 A new window may appear showing you the files being installed on your computer (see Figure 17.7), and you will be told when the installation process is complete.

Figure 17.7

7 You may find that a window containing QuickTime icons appears or you are told that QuickTime must be installed (see Figure 17.8). This program is needed for viewing your CD-ROM images and the latest version will be installed if it is not detected on your machine.

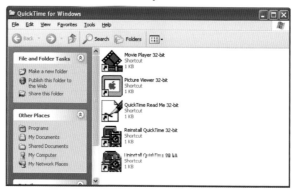

Figure 17.8

8 New programs sometimes include a shortcut that is placed on your desktop. Double-click this shortcut to start your program. Otherwise, you can find it from the **Start – All Programs** menu (see Figure 17.9). It may be under a general menu heading, and you need to click the correct icon to launch the program.

Figure 17.9

9 In most cases, not all the files will be installed on your machine, as they would take up too much space. You therefore need to keep the CD-ROM in the drive when using the program.

10 For each program, there will be indexes, menus and toolbars to learn how to use (see Figure 17.10). Some CD-ROMs are very well designed and seem straightforward, but in many cases it may take a while to understand the system. Resting the mouse pointer on parts of the screen should reveal tips and definitions, but, if it is too confusing, consult the Read Me file that is installed with the program.

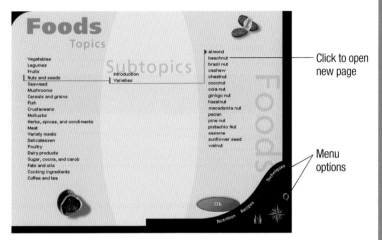

Foods

Topics

Subtopics

Vegetables
Legumes
Fruits
Nuts and seeds
Seaweed
Mushrooms
Cereals and grains
Fish
Crustaceans
Mollusks
Herbs, spices, and condiments
Meat
Variety meats
Delicatessen
Poultry
Dairy products
Sugar, cocoa, and carob
Fats and oils
Cooking ingredients
Coffee and tea

Introduction
Varieties

al mond
beechnut
brazil nut
cashew
chestnut
coconut
cola nut
ginkgo nut
hazelnut
macadamia nut
pecan
pine nut
pistachio Nut
sesame
sunflower seed
walnut

Click to open new page

Menu options

Ok

Nutrition   Recipes   Techniques

Figure 17.10

11. At some stage, you may decide you no longer want the program taking up space on your computer. Don't try to delete individual files, as you may remove shared files that are needed by other programs. Instead, locate the program folder from the **Start – All Programs** menu and select the **Uninstall** option (see Figure 17.11).

QuickTime
Startup
Ulead Photo Express 3.0 SE
Acer Aspire
Acrobat Reader 5.0

PictureViewer
QuickTime Player
QuickTime Updater
ReadMe
Uninstall QuickTime

Remove from computer

Figure 17.11

12. If this option is not available, open **Start – Control Panel** and select **Add or Remove Programs**. Locate the program in the list, select it and click **Change/Remove** (see Figure 17.12). All the files will be fully removed.

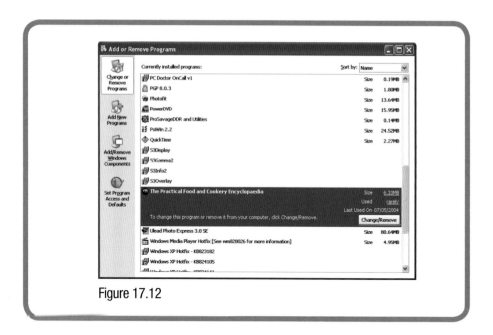

Figure 17.12

Appendix: Basic computing

The desktop

When you turn on your computer, after a few moments you will see your opening screen. This is the desktop. It will have a coloured background and will display the following basic items:

- **Icons** – small pictures will represent some parts of your computer, such as:

  - **the Recycle Bin** – where unwanted items are stored until removed completely;

  - **My Documents** – which is a folder in which you can store your work; and

  - **My Computer** – which provides access to everything in your machine.

- **Taskbar** – this is the bar running across the bottom of the screen. It is available wherever you are on your computer. It contains the green **Start** button that provides access to all your programs, and may also display different icons depending on how your machine has been set up. For example, Figure A.1 on the next page shows an icon for anti-virus checking software and a red cross next to a double computer symbol which means that the computer is not connected to the internet. The current time is also visible.

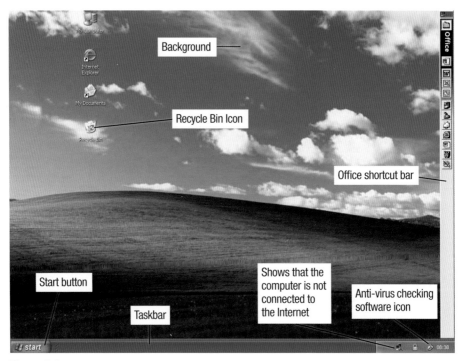

Figure A.1

Clicking the **Start** button opens the **Start** menu from which you can search for missing work, receive help on using your computer, open My Computer if it is not visible on the Desktop, change many of the computer settings, or connect to the internet.

If you have purchased Microsoft Office software, you may also see a shortcut to the various programs Office contains. It will be in the form of the Office Shortcut Bar running down the side of your screen or across the top.

Mouse

Most people are familiar with a keyboard, but mastering the mouse (the main method for giving instructions to the machine) can take a while. As you drag the mouse gently across the desk, it will move an arrow on the screen. This is the pointer.

- **To select** – position the pointer over any object and press down the left mouse button briefly before letting go. This is known as *clicking*. If you click an icon on the desktop, it changes colour. If you click a menu, a list of options appears, and if you click in a box you confirm an action such as closing or deleting.

- **To open** – you can use the mouse to open an icon if you click the left mouse button twice, very fast. This is ***double-clicking***. An alternative is to select the object with one click and then press the Enter key on the keyboard.

- **To move/drag** – position the pointer over an object, press down the left button and hold it down as you drag the mouse across the screen.

- **Shortcut menu** – if you click the right mouse button on any part of the screen, you will open a short menu of relevant options. To choose one, click it once with the left mouse button. The chosen option usually changes colour.

Windows

Each object on the desktop, and all the programs you will be using, can be opened up. They will appear inside a window and, although each program will have its own special tools, the basic structure and management of these windows is very similar.

- **Title bar** – this shows the program you are using and the name of the piece of work. It is untitled until your work is saved (see Chapter 1).

- **Minimise button** – click this to keep your work open but out of the way – it will be 'parked' on the taskbar and can be restored with one click.

- **Maximise button** – click this to expand the window to fill the entire screen. It is best to work with a maximised window, as all the tools will be fully available.

- **Restore Down button** – (alternates with **Maximise**) – click this to reduce the size of your window if you want to see other programs or the desktop behind. Several windows can be open at the same time, and the top, active, window will obscure the others. Reach them quickly by restoring down the top one. You can also move a window, by dragging, only when it is restored down.

- **Close button** – click this to close the window. You will be reminded if you have not yet saved your work.

- **Scroll bars** – these appear on the right and bottom of the window if the contents are too big to view. Click the arrow in the appropriate direction to move across or down the page.

Menus

Each program will have some basic options to help you organise and edit your work, as well as specific menus related to the actual program (for example, the drawing package Paint has colour and image menus that are not available when word processing). All programs have a:

- **Help** menu – offering advice on carrying out the tasks
- **File** menu – from which to save, print or open a saved piece of work
- **Edit** menu – for deleting or copying parts of the work
- **View** menu – in case you need to zoom in or out to see certain areas in more detail.

Dialog box

When you make a selection from a menu, you often open a new window known as a **_dialog box_**. This may offer different 'pages' in the form of **_tabs_** that you click, and will display a range of options available either by typing in, clicking a down-facing arrow, or clicking small radio buttons or check boxes. Sometimes there are up and down arrows to increase or decrease measurements or numbers.

Help

Whenever you are stuck and cannot remember, or find out, how to do something, you should open the **Help** menu. This offers general introductions to topics via a Contents list, an alphabetical search through all the major topics covered via the Index, and a more specific keyword search using the Search function. Click an option in the left-hand pane and read the guidance or follow the demonstration offered on the right.

In most applications, you will also find a question box in the top, right-hand corner. Type in a question and press the Enter key to link up to the appropriate help text. Click the most relevant point to open the help screen.

Glossary

Accessing	Finding and opening a web page.
Active cell	The cell showing a black border, in which any data will appear when you type text or numbers. You activate a new cell by clicking in it with the mouse or moving there by pressing the Tab, Enter or arrow keys.
Active window	When more than one window is open at the same time, this is the only window with a blue title bar in which you are able to work.
Application	The named software that is dedicated to a related group of tasks, such as word processing or drawing (eg Microsoft Word or Microsoft Publisher).
Bitmap file	A graphics (picture) file created when using an application such as Microsoft Paint and made up of a collection of coloured dots known as pixels.
Bookmarking	Storing a favourite web page address so that it can be opened again easily.
Browser	The application that allows you to view web pages on the world wide web (www).
Browsing	(see Surfing)
CD-ROMs	Shiny round disks placed on the slide-out tray in your computer that contain applications, such as encyclopaedias, games, drawing packages or music.
Cells	Squares in tables or spreadsheets where you enter your data.
Central Processing Unit (CPU)	The heart of your computer that controls its main functions.
Chat room	A special kind of website where you can communicate in writing with other people online at the same time.
Clicking	Pressing a button on your mouse to instruct the computer to carry out a particular task.

Clipboard	An area of the computer memory where you temporarily store text or images before moving or copying them to another file or within the same file.
Compressing files	(see *Zipping*)
Cursor	A flashing black bar that marks the text insertion point.
Database	Information about people or things stored in a systematic way that can be sorted or searched.
Default	Settings for your work or the equipment you are using that are selected automatically and can be accepted or changed manually.
Desktop	The opening screen you see when you turn on your computer. Its name derives from the various little pictures you see that represent items in an office, such as a wastepaper basket (the Recycle Bin).
Dialog box	Small window (opened via a menu) that offers you various choices to click or type in.
Digital camera	Equipment that creates digital photographs that can be viewed and stored on the computer.
Domain name	Parts of a web address that display an organisation's registered name, location and type of business.
Double-clicking	Clicking the left mouse button twice very fast. It is used as a quick method to open programs or files and can be replaced by selecting the item with one click of the left mouse button and then pressing the Enter key on the keyboard.
Downloading	Transferring files from the internet onto your own computer.
Drive	Slot in the computer housing a disk and usually referred to by letter; for example, the C: drive (for the hard disk) or A: drive (for a floppy disk).
Driver	Software program needed to operate hardware such as printers, modems, graphics cards, scanners and cameras.

Email	Electronic messages sent via the internet.
Fieldname	The heading or category under which information in a database is stored.
File	Piece of work – text, numbers, images or other objects – created and saved onto a computer.
File type/extension	Part of a file name showing the application used to produce it or what type of file it is.
Floppy disk	A thin disk encased in a square or rectangular plastic shell used for storing information. Today's computers generally do not have floppy drives built in; older computers will have the facility to take floppy disks.
Folder	Labelled space where you can store related programs and files.
Font	Type of character used when typing text or numbers.
Formula	Instructions to the computer to carry out a calculation.
Forum	*(see Social network)*
Function	Instructions recognised by a spreadsheet application to perform specific calculations.
Function keys	Keys along the top of the keyboard that do not relate to any characters but act as shortcuts to various actions; for example, opening the Help menu (F1) or checking spelling (F7).
Gateway	Website that can be searched for links to other sites on a single theme (eg education, health).
Greyscale	View of a picture that shows shades of grey instead of colours.
Hard disk	Main area within the computer on which programs and files are stored.
Hardware	Parts of the computer you can see and touch.
Help	Demonstrations, explanations and other assistance available when working on your computer.
Hyperlink	Text or pictures that are embedded in web pages and can be clicked to open related pages.

Icons	Small pictures representing programs or shortcuts to common tasks.
Internet	Computers around the world that are linked and can share information.
ISP (Internet Service Provider)	The organisation that supplies software and facilities to allow you to link to the internet and send emails.
IT (Information Technology)	The technical term for using technology to communicate and handle information.
Jpeg file	A type of graphics file that is recognised by a browser so that pictures (often photographs) can be displayed on the web. The other common web graphics file format is a gif file.
Junk mail	*(see Spam)*
Justify	Text is spread across the page to 'neaten' its appearance on the right-hand margin.
Keywords	Any important words or phrases typed into a query/search box that form the basis of a search for relevant records or websites.
Log in	Entering your personal name and password to access secure areas on a computer.
Marquee	Dotted lines showing a selected area.
Megapixels	(see *Resolution*)
Message board	(see *Social networks*)
Modem	The hardware required to allow digital computer information to travel down standard telephone lines.
Mouse	Hardware that allows you to move a pointer on screen and click a button to instruct the computer to carry out a particular task.
Newsgroups	Groups of people with a common interest who communicate via email.
Online/offline	Connected or disconnected from the internet.
Operating system	Software controlling the general operation of the computer.
Optical Character Recognition (OCR)	The technology that allows typewritten material to be scanned into a computer in the form of a word-processed document.

Orientation	The setting you select that determines how a page is printed – either upright (portrait), or turned sideways (landscape) so that the longer sides are top and bottom.
Package	*(see Application)*
PC (Personal Computer)	The type of computer that sits on your desk at home or work and contains most of the programs and files you use.
PDF (Portable Document Format)	A popular way for documents to be distributed on the web, as they retain all their formatting and layout.
Placeholder	An area already in place on a slide where you can insert different objects, such as charts or pictures.
Programs	Ordered sets of instructions that the computer carries out.
RAM (Random Access Memory)	The memory your computer uses to open and run the different applications.
Relational database	An application that allows you to search for related data across a number of tables of information.
Resolution	The sharpness of a picture. Resolution is measured in millions of pixels ('dots') known as megapixels.
Scanner	Equipment used to transfer text or images from paper into a computer.
Search engine	A website that holds a vast database of web pages that you search using keywords.
Server	A remote computer in a networked system that houses the network operating system software along with any software applications and data files that need to be shared.
Shareware	Programs or files on the world wide web (www) that are either free or very cheap to use.
Shortcut	A way of carrying out common tasks without needing to go through the menu options. Common shortcuts are available within each application by clicking toolbar buttons at the top of the screen.

Social network (or forum or message board)	A cross between emailing a large group of people and pinning up notices on a notice board.
Software	The instructions, in the form of programs, that the computer needs to be able to work effectively.
Spam (or junk mail)	Unsolicited emails.
Spreadsheet	Text labels and numerical data created using a program that can perform calculations.
Surfing (or browsing)	Describes the activity of searching the internet for information.
Task pane	An optional sidebar that appears within Office XP applications offering shortcuts to related activitioc.
Taskbar	The bar along the bottom of the screen that is always available and that houses the Start button, some general information such as the time and date, any minimised files and shortcuts to some of your applications or controls.
Template	A file that is used to create a variety of different files based on its contents and style but that is left unaltered.
TFT	The technology used to create computer monitor screens that are thin and flat and take up far less room than normal desktop monitors.
Toolbar	Rows of buttons that act as shortcuts to the more common activities carried out when using your computer. Each toolbar contains a set of buttons related to a particular group of tasks, such as Drawing or Tables.
URL (Uniform Resource Locator)	The address of any web page.
Username	Your identifying name for logging in, or as part of your email address.
Virus	A rogue program that damages your files and is 'caught' via the internet or from infected floppy disks.

Web page	Documents containing text, pictures, sounds, moving images etc, written in code (usually HTML), that are stored on computers around the world and can be viewed when you connect to the internet.
Website	A collection of linked web pages found at the same address and created by a single organisation.
Wizards	Guides found in various Microsoft applications that can help you produce files or objects step-by-step.
Workbook	The name given to files created in Microsoft Excel. Each workbook contains a number of sheets that are saved with the file.
World wide web (known as the web or www)	All the multimedia web pages displayed in a browser window when you connect to the internet.
Zipping	Reducing the size of files so that they take up less room and can be sent more easily by email or stored on disk.

Index

About Age Concern

Age Concern is the UK's largest organisation working for and with older people to enable them to make more of life. We are a federation of over 400 independent charities who share the same name, values and standards and believe that later life should be fulfilling, enjoyable and productive.

Age Concern Books

Age Concern publishes a wide range of bestselling books that help thousands of people each year. They provide practical, trusted advice on subjects ranging from pensions and planning for retirement, to using a computer and surfing the internet. Whether you are caring for someone with a health problem or want to know more about your rights to healthcare, we have something for everyone.

Ordering is easy

To order any of our books or request our free catalogue simply choose one of the following options:

- Call us on 0870 44 22 120
- Visit our website at www.ageconcern.org.uk/bookshop
- Email us at sales@ageconcernbooks.co.uk

You can also buy our books from all good bookshops.

Age Concern England
1268 London Road
London
SW16 4ER
Tel: 020 8765 7200
www.ageconcern.org.uk

Age Concern Cymru
Ty John Pathy
Units 13 and 14 Neptune Court
Vanguard Way
Cardiff CF24 5PJ
Tel: 029 2043 1555
www.accymru.org.uk

Age Concern Scotland
Causewayside House
160 Causewayside
Edinburgh EH9 1PP
Tel: 0845 833 0200
www.ageconcernscotland.org.uk

Age Concern Northern Ireland
3 Lower Crescent
Belfast
BT7 1NR
Tel: 028 9024 5729
www.ageconcernni.org

More Great Books From Age Concern...

Feeling good!

Easy steps to staying healthy
Dr Alan Maryon Davis

Winner of Medical Journalists' Association Health and Journalism in the Media award 2008

'This book is a joy. Alan Maryon Davis sings with humorous group Instant Sunshine, and he uses his comedic talents to inform in the most lively and accessible way. This book should sell and sell for generations.'
Comments from MJA Awards 2008

Written by well-known media medic, Dr Alan Maryon Davis, and illustrated by Quentin Blake, this is a must have self-help guide providing a light-hearted, yet serious, approach to the secrets of keeping fit and healthy for longer. It pulls together all the crucial health and fitness facts that you and your loved ones might ignore at your peril. It busts the common myths that many blindly follow and covers the 10 key lifestyle areas that can dramatically improve health including:

- Diet & nutrition • Physical activity • Stress • Relaxation & sleep • Sex
- Smoking • Drinking and drugs • Oral health • Skincare & sunbathing
  • How to develop a positive approach to life

£9.99 • Paperback • 978-0-86242-423-7

Your rights: working after 50

A guide to your employment options
Andrew Harrop & Susie Munro

The definitive guide to getting the most out of work after 50 so you, not other people, decide when you're ready to stop work. Ensure you know your rights in the workplace, learn about support if you're out of work, and find out about the many career opportunities available, from setting up your own business to updating your skills and remaining competitive. Contents include:

- Age discrimination at work • Self-employment
- Updating your skills and remaining competitive
- CV and interview techniques • Training and support services
  • Dispute resolution

£8.99 • Paperback • 978-086242-425-1

Your rights to healthcare, 2nd edition

Helping older people get the best from the NHS
Lorna Easterbrook

Do you know your way round the NHS? This complete guide explains what NHS services you are entitled to as well as what to do – and what to expect – when you come into contact with the health service. It provides clear and up-to-date information on areas such as opticians, dentists, GPs, hospitals and support for long-term illness. Although written for older people, the advice offered could benefit anyone using the NHS in England.

Issues also covered include:

- Going into and coming out of hospital • Mental health
- NHS care where you live • Organ and blood donation
- Making complaints • Useful addresses

£7.99 • Paperback • 978-086242-422-0

Ordering is easy

To order any of our books or request our free catalogue simply choose one of the following options:

- Call us on 0870 44 22 120
- Visit our website at www.ageconcern.org.uk/bookshop
- Email us at orders@acil.org.uk

You can also buy our books from all good bookshops.